Making Loss Matter

Making Loss Matter

Creating
Meaning in
Difficult
Times

Rabbi David Wolpe

Riverhead Books

a member of Penguin Putnam Inc.

New York

1999

RIVERHEAD BOOKS
a member of
Penguin Putnam Inc.
375 Hudson Street
New York, NY 10014

Library of Congress Cataloging-in-Publication Data
Wolpe, David J.
Making loss matter : creating meaning in difficult times /
by David Wolpe.
p.   cm.
ISBN 1-57322-141-4
1. Loss (Psychology)—Religious aspects—Judaism.
2. Consolation (Judaism)   3. Bereavement—Religious aspects—Judaism.
4. Wolpe, David J.—Religion.   5. Jewish way of life.   I. Title.
BM729.C6W65   1999
296.3'118 — dc21   99-20677 CIP

Printed in the United States of America

1   3   5   7   9   10   8   6   4   2

This book is printed on acid-free paper. ∞

Book design by Chris Welch

1999

In memory of
Sarah and Abraham Ring
and
Sally and Benjamin Wolpe

Contents

Foreword

A few years ago, I wrote a book called *Tuesdays with Morrie,* the story of my old college professor whom I visited weekly when he was dying from Lou Gehrig's disease. Before that book, I was never asked to write forewords; no one thought me worthy. Now, after *Tuesdays with Morrie,* I find myself declining a great deal of foreword invitations. This time, the party who thinks I am unworthy is me.

I make the exception here because, first of all, this is an exceptional book. Second, it is written by a friend. David Wolpe wasn't always a rabbi when I knew him. He wasn't always a learned scholar, or a celebrated author, although he has become all those things. But he was always a friend.

We met as eleven-year-olds, in a musty classroom during an entrance exam for a private school. We were seated next to one another, and, as happens in nervous situations like that, we bonded through a few brief minutes of conversation. I liked him. I think he liked me. We quickly became, for each other, "the only kid I know in this room." When the tests started, we put our heads down in shared concentration.

Next thing I knew, David was turning his test in and waving good-bye. I watched him go—my paper was not yet half completed. I barely knew him, but when he waved, a voice inside me gave a plaintive whisper: *"Hey. Where you going?"* I suppose you could say, then, our relationship began with a loss. I was sure I had lost a new friend; David probably figured he had lost a kid too dumb to finish the test. But, as fate would have it, we met again, six months later, on the first day of school. Both of us had made the grade (though obviously at different speeds). When we spotted each other, we slapped each other's backs like old friends.

Lost. Then found.

I lost David again, six years later. I graduated high school and went away—to Brandeis University, and my beloved teacher, Morrie Schwartz—while David remained in Philadelphia, studying at Penn. Our correspondence dwindled. We got involved with new people. The halls we wandered were no longer places we could bump into one another.

Although David and I had been great buddies in high school—sleeping over at each other's houses, sharing sports stories, demonstrating our driving skills when we each got our licenses—the few times I saw him during college, it was clear we were drifting apart. David, at the time, wanted to be a lawyer. I had dreams of being a musician. By the time we graduated, we weren't even close enough to phone and offer congratulations. Now and then, I would hear about what David was doing, and I lamented our vanished kinship. That same inner voice would moan quietly, *"Hey. Where you going?"*

Lost. Found. Lost.

I traveled, gave up music, took up journalism, and found a

home in writing. David traveled, gave up law, took up the rabbinate, and found a home in Judaica. And one day, that simply,
we reconnected. Maybe it was a phone call. A visit. Maybe it
was David's wedding, in California, when we stole a few minutes away from the celebration and shared our disbelief that we
had grown so old as to take on wives.

Anyhow, our relationship was rekindled, now as adults—lost,
found, lost, found—and while I pondered the fate of our culture through the eyes of a reporter, David pondered it through
the eyes of a man often looked to for fixing it. This, as you might
imagine, has made for some wonderful discussions. It has also
drawn us to some similar conclusions. One of those is the basic
premise of this book: that all of life is a series of losses, which,
if woven correctly from the sadness, can stitch a richer emotional fabric of our days.

David and I are not the first to reach this conclusion. Not
hardly. A famous rabbi once said, "The only whole heart is a broken one"; Tennyson wrote that it is better to have loved and lost;
and Michael Jordan made a TV commercial on how the setbacks
in his life have made him a winner. If you can connect Judaism,
Tennyson, and Nike, you are not standing on a newly discovered line. But what David does so magnificently in this book is
take the idea and make it real. He writes, through a wonderful
blend of religious annotation and personal experience, of the
loss we suffer through death, its most painful form. But he also
details the smaller losses of life—losing our first homes, losing
our youthful dreams, losing ourselves in the wayward sways of
adulthood—and explains how each of these unfolding losses
teaches us to grow and to go on, changed, perhaps, but also
stronger and wiser.

The beauty of *Making Loss Matter* is that it is not pop psychology, nor is it one man's dogmatic view of grief and suffering. Rather, this is a book that calls upon vast references, from the Bible to Proust to Somerset Maugham. Interspersed are the real-life experiences David has encountered as a teacher, father, husband, and comforter of souls. One gets the feeling reading this book that its conclusions have been earned with time and compassion.

That David, a wise and respected rabbi, should be an author to expound on loss is, of course, perfectly natural. Don't we always turn to our religious leaders when we suffer a loss? Are they not the ones whose arms we enter, whose soothing embrace we seek, whose eyes we look into when we hear that wailing cry, *"Hey. Where are they going?"*

I remember, as a child, being in awe at the rabbis and priests who stood at rain-soaked grave sites and delivered inspiring eulogies, blankets so comforting that we could not think of placing our loved ones in the ground without them. But I also remember a time, as a young man, when my family gathered to bury an uncle. He was a favorite of mine, a tough, irascible guy who was as gritty as his whiskers. The cleric at the funeral parlor did not know him well, and when he began his eulogy, he mispronounced his last name. I seethed inside. My uncle did not take kindly to strangers, and the thought of him making his curtain call under a stranger's tongue burned my stomach with an unsettling urge. Finally, when the cleric was done, I asked if I could speak.

And I did. I spoke from the heart. From memories. From love. I had never delivered a eulogy before, but I spoke about the man in that coffin and my voice broke and I began to cry. Still, I kept speaking, the words gurgling out in spurts of breath. It was a messy, tear-soaked thing, but when it was finished, I felt right. I felt at peace. There was a need to face the loss and to get my arms around it. When I embraced it, I actually felt better, not worse.

I believe that is what David is onto here, that there is something therapeutic and healthy in learning to make loss matter. I believe it is a critical message, the same one I heard at my old professor's deathbed, when Morrie held my hand and said, "Remember, death ends a life, but not a relationship."

So it is with all loss. Something ends, but something continues. Lost. Found. Lost. Found. In writing this little foreword, I was reminded of the 1984 funeral of my beloved grandmother, who had lived with us for most of my childhood. My family, too devastated to speak, wanted someone to eulogize her in a personal way. Someone she knew. We chose a young rabbinical student named David Wolpe, who used to tease her in Yiddish when we were kids. And he spoke wonderfully, a farewell that balanced the loss of the moment with the gains of a lifetime. On that day, in a very dark moment, he offered a beacon. What he never told me—and I didn't know until a phone call today—was that it was his first eulogy.

So obviously, from the start, he's had a feel for the resonance of loss. In *Making Loss Matter,* through a mix of scholarship, pathos, anecdote, and personal experience, David Wolpe— Rabbi and friend—now takes on this most crucial subject with the healing hands of a teacher. And once again, as in that old musty classroom, I gaze with awe at his completed task.

Mitch Albom
Detroit, Michigan
May 1, 1999

One

Making Loss Matter

I will build an altar from the broken fragments of my heart.
—Yehuda HeChasid

*I*n high school I read a book by the late Ernest Becker entitled *The Denial of Death*. It is a profound and beautiful work, and I have reread it more than once. The book describes the strategies, good and bad, that we use to deny or evade the fact that we all one day will die. Remarkably, as he was completing his book about death and how we cope with it, Becker discovered that he was dying.

I thought of that many times as I struggled with this book. For as I was writing about loss, not only did I experience loss, but nearly every day, people approached me with tales of loss.

While working on the chapter about the loss of dreams, I had lunch with a man named George Smith. George is a successful businessman. He and his wife, Pam, have a daughter, Rebecca. When Rebecca was a baby, George and Pam noticed that she had a balance problem. At first they did not imagine it was serious, but in time they brought her to a doctor, who diagnosed

her with a mild form of cerebral palsy. A few years later, however, when Rebecca was five years old, they discovered that she
had ataxia telangiectasia (AT), a degenerative disease that is ultimately fatal.

I had lunch with George because I was going to speak at a
large annual luncheon he and Pam host each year to raise money
for AT research. He and his wife had built a charity, and a net-
work, that is astonishing. When George and Pam began their
work, this rare disease was virtually ignored. Now it is the subject of a major research effort.

Caring for someone with AT is a full-time job. Rebecca is
about to turn twenty-one, which is very old for someone
afflicted with this disease. She is confined to a wheelchair and
has several disabilities. Each day she and her family live with too
many losses to count.

When George and Pam first received confirmation of their
daughter's diagnosis, Pam turned to her husband and said,
"Today we bury the child we thought we had, and give birth to
a new child."

In that sentence is much of the wisdom of love and loss. First,
there is in that phrase the realism that puts aside old hopes and
dreams. Becky would not play like other children. She would
not live easily and thoughtlessly in her body like her classmates.
But the death of that dream was not the death of all their dreams.
It was the birth of another dream, more difficult, perhaps, but
not without its own special rewards and joys. Looking out over
the 1,500 people at the luncheon, one could feel how rich
Rebecca had made her parents' lives.

Shortly after my first encounter with Rebecca, I met with a
man whose botched surgery left him, in his thirties, disabled for

life; I counseled a woman who was carrying a child that genetic testing showed would have serious life problems; after I gave a sermon on the importance of honesty, a young woman introduced herself and told me she had cancer, and asked whether she should talk about that at first meetings in order to be honest.

Each of these people was searching less for techniques of coping than for deeper lessons, deeper meaning. "In the evening there will be weeping, but in the morning, joy," sang the Psalmist (Psalms 30:6). Through the lens of loss, those men and women to whom I spoke were looking for the colors that make life richer, more beautiful.

I was not "called" to become a rabbi. Friends of mine—rabbis, ministers, priests—felt a compulsion to enter the clergy. It was part of them. They were spiritual from the start. Not me.

I entered the rabbinate in part because I was afraid of what I might otherwise have done. I was an ambitious kid, and my ambition could have found many other outlets. I was wild, with appetites and dreams that are not of the kind you want in your rabbi. My wife and I once unpacked an old box of pictures from my college days. There are photos of me with friends, and she wanted me to throw them away so that our daughter would not grow up to see them. They are snapshots of carousing, unsuitable for a rabbi. I tucked them back in the box and hid them away.

Becoming a rabbi was a way to foster the best in me. Of course, I know rabbis and other clergy who violate the codes they preach. But, in my experience, that violation troubles them, even tortures them. They cannot let it go, because they know they opted to seek something higher. But to live a spiritual life is not easy for me. Sometimes I think that it was not for being a rabbi that I was born.

Though we are given selves, we also shape them. I took my recalcitrance and made a rabbi out of it. And I did it largely because of loss.

People I knew as I grew up had lost children, parents, siblings, spouses, careers, homes, hopes. My father told me how his own father's death, when my father was eleven, had marked him for life; in the telling, he impressed the presence of loss on me. I used to imagine my father as a young boy, hearing the news that his father had died. I pictured him running to his mother in the middle of the night, the night after his father's funeral, screaming because the pelting rain outside would drown his father, who was buried in the ground. I remember vividly his telling me how he used to go to an uncle's house to hear him talk and sing—his uncle's voice sounded like the voice of his own father so much that it brought his father back to him. One day, my father told me, he went to his uncle's house, but all he could hear was his uncle. His father's voice had been lost.

While I studied in rabbinical school, my mother suffered a stroke that stole her speech. She was fifty-two years old. One day my mother was poised and able, a university administrator and teacher. The next day she was fighting for her life. The disabilities from the stroke would ease somewhat, but life had been wrenched from the tracks and would never be the same.

A favorite piece of clothing wears out and must be discarded; an old store closes; the month changes. Things we treasured early in life have faded and do not echo in the consciousness of those who are younger. Musicians we loved for their youth and anger appear as contented middle-aged men with bellies where their angst used to be. Friends we thought would always be by our side live far away, and occasionally the phone rings to remind us that once we were bound up in each other's lives. We remember the block we grew up on, a place of baseball games and tall stories, of confidences and tears. When we return in later years, or take our children to see it, it has turned into a parking lot, an office building, or has become so run-down that the magic of our memory seems a dream.

Some of these losses may be trivial, but they kick up the old motif in our minds—that time slowly strips the world of things we care about and things we love. We are the citizens not only of the present but of what one poet called the land of lost content: "those happy highways where I went and cannot go again."

My ninety-year-old grandmother told me shortly before she died, "David, build up memories. One day it will be all you have to live on."

Sooner or later every one of us becomes an expert on loss. Several years ago I watched a television interview with an elderly woman whose friends had died. When the interviewer asked what she missed most, this dignified woman said in a steady voice, "There is no one to call me Rosie anymore." Her nickname was lost with the last of her friends. Her world had grown colder.

When people die, we mourn them. Societies develop intricate ritualized systems for comforting those who mourn the death of family and friends. But what of other things that die? How do we mourn them, understand them? Why is this world built so that the seasons of life are shot through with autumn?

There is no magic answer to loss. Nothing, not even time, will make the pain completely disappear. But loss is transformative if it is met with faith. Faith is our chance to make sense of loss, to cope with the stone that rolls around in the hollow of our stomachs when something we loved, something we thought was forever, is suddenly gone.

In recent years we have turned to psychology to enhance our understanding of life's losses. But the human struggle is not simply a product of training and genetics. Our tragedies and dreams are not adequately explained by probing childhood or even imagination. Unless we see ourselves as spiritual beings—as well as social and psychological beings—we shall never truly advance in our understanding of humanity. In times of grief we need to deal with the unreasonable, and only traditions that speak directly to the human soul will guide us through.

For most of human history, the discipline of psychology was not separate from religion. Our ancestors had to deal with the losses of life, but they did not turn to therapy. Instead the generations before us looked to the oldest reservoirs of human wisdom—religious traditions. Their understandings were shaped not only by intuition but also by rich traditions that stretched back as far as memory. In the struggles of characters told in epic poetry and sacred scripture they saw their own struggles. As the Jewish tradition puts it, "The actions of the ancestors are signposts to their descendants."

A religious tradition sees loss differently than other disciplines. A great religious tradition has its own vocabulary and insight.

Psychology is a miner who seeks to unearth the rich and raw data of the mind. Religion is a miner, too, but also a mountaineer. It climbs above the human mind to understand it. Spiritual psychology bases itself on the idea that there is something outside ourselves without which we cannot understand ourselves. There is in the universe a cohering force that makes our efforts worthy and our losses meaningful. Repairing the breaches in human spirit is a task of reaching not only inward but upward.

A great religious tradition does not deny the pain of loss. In the words of the Kotzker Rebbe, "The only whole heart is a broken one." No awake spirit can move through this world without enduring a broken heart. There is nothing real that makes life painless. Accepting the pain of living, knowing one's heart will—and should—be broken, is the beginning of wisdom.

Years ago in a memorial service, my father, who is also a rabbi, gave a sermon about how faithful we are to remember those who have died, but how neglectful we are, at times, about things that die while we are still alive: relationships, dreams, loves. I was very touched by the idea, reworked it, and gave a sermon on the same theme. The response from the congregation was overwhelming. Everyone sitting in that service had suffered some loss. They all wondered how to come to grips with a world in which loss is unending. A friend suggested I expand the idea, deepen it, and write this book. The task proved to be much harder than I had thought.

This book has been rewritten many times. The first draft was an exercise in intellect, filled with citations, more a learned treatise than a book about loss. All my life I have been a reader; I read compulsively—in planes, at the breakfast table, on line in the supermarket and post office, in bed, in front of the TV, and everywhere else. Sometimes reading returns me to myself; sometimes it takes me away. But the theme of loss did not unfold itself to me as I read. Maybe the idea was too painful for me to confront directly, so I hid behind what this writer said, or what that scholar thought. I was safe, but the book was far from my heart.

After I had done some research, after I had immersed myself in the reflections of others, I put the books and magazines and journals down. For one summer I stayed away from the piles of print in my office and on my bed stand. I did not fill my head with the truths that others had written. Finally I consulted how I felt, in addition to what I thought. I spoke with people I knew who had suffered and who had made it through. The pages that follow are filled with the stories and words of others, from both my readings and my conversations. Often they express what I wish to say more deeply than I could unaided. But I had to write this book from my heart, not only for myself, but for the losses of those whom I know, those whom I knew, and those whom I love. No one lives without loss. One can live without *truly* living, because loss is so painful and paralyzing. But it comes nonetheless, early and late.

A year and a half after I began this book, nine months after our daughter was born, my wife was diagnosed with cancer. The ordeal began routinely, with a phone call from a doctor about a test that looked suspicious. Soon we were stunned by the reality that Eliana was very sick.

At every stage I believed the best. It would prove not to be cancer. It would be mild. It would not affect our ability to have more children. Successively, these hopes were dashed.

Eliana had always been healthy. The sudden upending of our lives—with a new baby, having just moved across the country—spun us around and loosed our bearings. We consulted various doctors to get as much information as possible. Eliana hurriedly pumped breast milk so that the baby would not have to be weaned when she was in the hospital. Family and friends offered their help. Life was suddenly full of shadows.

That experience colors this book as it does our lives. The texture of it will always remain with me: the smell of the hospital, the nights apart, the hours of surgery, the moment when Eliana woke up and held my hand. Equally, some of the currents that ran beneath those moments stay with me: the speed with which life turns around, the fragility of all we love, the courage required to keep heart, and the way a loss can recede but never disappears.

Preachers often have claimed to have the answer to why the world is so constructed that we lose what we love. The answer is often beautiful, and even convincing, until loss strikes. Then it fades like the clouds at evening; the dark wipes out the beauty. Losses are the stuff of life. They will not miss you, they will not steer around those whom you love.

We search for an answer to the riddle of "why" because we want control. Give us a way to make sure that we will not lose again. But God gives this privilege to no one.

As I came to understand this quest, I began a quest of my own—not for an answer, but for an approach.

I was not searching for a why but for a how: How do I make this loss meaningful? Its origin was a mystery. What would be its end? Could I , with the powers of my own hand and heart, with the help of those whom I love, turn a painful, inexplicable loss into a generator of purpose and of hope, even of blessing?

These are not new questions; they are recurrent questions. When religion turns from them and becomes an explainer rather than a creator, it loses its central mission. The central mission of religion is not to answer questions.

Life is not an intellectual puzzle. Life is a precious, one-time chance to grow. We grow not by solving riddles but by creating meaning.

Loss is not an issue in crisis alone. We lose at each moment of life. Each morning as I leave for work, I am losing time I could be spending with my family. That is irreplaceable time, and it has a special poignancy to me. Like in a game show, we can choose what is behind only one of the three doors. All life is limited, and limitation means loss. I have lost other lives I might have had. We all have. Most of the time we see the blessing of the choices we make. But then a moment creeps in, a daydream instant, when we muse about what we might have been or what we might be, if only the rules of time's passing were not so severe, so certain.

Change is the passing away of one state and the coming into being of another. Loss is one of the faces of change. Without loss we would live in a steady-state world, a world where progress is stilled.

To know this fact is not to welcome it. We know things must change, and we are glad. Still, that does not mean that we can bear the particular changes that life sometimes brings. We know that people must die. We do not accept that *this* person must die, surely not at *this* time. The knowledge that change is inevitable does not lighten the sadness.

When I was first ordained as a rabbi, I spent some time tutoring a man who was in prison. He had been fabulously rich and quite famous, and now he had been stripped of most of his wealth. During part of his day he cleaned milk cartons. As prisons go, it was a nice place, but still he was strip-searched when I left, and his life still was in the charge of other people twenty-four hours a day. The humiliation was almost as painful as physical discomfort would have been. From his exalted perch to even a "country club" prison was a breathtaking drop.

We were studying theology. Was there nothing, he wondered, that could explain what had happened? To say he committed a crime was not enough. The dimensions of the difference—from tycoon to convict— cried out for something more comprehensive. He had lost so much—his position, his wealth, and eventually his marriage—that there had to be a note of wisdom in our tradition to explain his loss.

The man's dilemma haunts us all, in each person's individual life. Sometimes, as with a prisoner, we can trace the sequence of events and understand what led to loss. But almost as often, the losses in life seem arbitrary, hard to fit into any pattern.

In what follows we will examine different kinds of losses: of love, of dreams, of home, of youth, of life, and more. The themes keep recurring; the loss is real and painful. Yet the Divine project for humanity is growth, and that requires the conviction of meaning. Despair, said Rabbi Nachman of Bratzlav, is the greatest sin. Despair is the collapse of hope. To despair is to believe that God's world is ultimately bleak and dark. Loss is a

constant temptation to despair. Faith is, if not the antidote, at
least the counteragent.

The first comment God makes about human beings in the Bible
is: "It is not good for man to be alone" (Gen. 2:18). We fear loss
in part because we fear being alone. A person alone is like a
splinter chipped off the carpenter's block, without connection
to something greater. Behind all the little anxieties of each loss
is the shuddering fear of losing everything we care for, everyone we love. A loss makes us feel, inside, less connected.

Loss drives us to create even as it reminds us that all creation
is ephemeral. Part of the invariable lesson of loss is that without
it, one remains a child. I once spoke to a group of recovering
alcoholics. We talked about Jacob's dream in the Bible, about
dreams realized and shattered. One man told me that when he
stopped drinking at the age of forty, he realized that he had the
maturity of an eighteen-year-old. At eighteen he began to drink
to anesthetize himself, and he had felt no pain since that time.
Without pain he did not grow, and so at forty, he was still eighteen. Now that he was sober, he was feeling the pain of life
again, and his spiritual age was catching up with his chrono-
logical age.

The blessing we seek in life is not to live without pain. It is
to live so that our pain has meaning. The spiritually mindful person seeks to live fully despite fear, because to allow fear to direct
our lives adds the suffering of anticipation to the pain of the loss.
No quality is more essential for a well-lived life than courage.
Loss is arbitrary; our valor in living, and our determination to

make sense of life, is wisdom. As my friend Linda said about her illness, "I am going to live with the fear, and I am going to *really* live in spite of it."

When I was a child learning to swim, I had a hard time floating. I was too afraid of drowning, and I knew that by thrashing my arms and legs I could usually manage to keep my head above water. Learning to float is learning to trust the world, and oneself. Paradoxically, though, it is by floating, by not being afraid, that the wave carries us highest. Sometimes when I floated, the wave covered me, just as it did when I thrashed about. But in between waves I was no longer afraid, and when the wave washed over me, I knew I would soon again ride the crest.

Each person of courage must face the world, a joyous and fearful and hope-filled place. We will lose what we love, but we will have loved. We will reach, and falter. The ocean will not engulf us. We will hold one another and realize that in God's world, none need be alone.

> Light is known to exist by virtue of darkness. . . . One is the chair upon which the other sits.
>
> —Rabbi Aharon of Apt

The question of making meaning is constantly before all of us in different ways. In the life of a rabbi, loss is never very far. In one day I spoke with several people whose lives were altered in an instant. One man I did not know called me to relate that his doctor told him he had to lose his teeth. He is a vital, thoughtful man. Suddenly, he felt old. His teeth were symbolic of something more, of the vigor of youth. He did not have to think when he ate. A toothless mouth felt to him more like a question of destiny than dentistry. It scared him, and he felt the loss.

Earlier in that morning, I had met with a grandparent whose grandchild was very sick. She wanted to speak to the child, who was in his early teens, about his illness in a way that would be meaningful. She saw that the child was looking to her for answers—and she had no answers. She had only sadness.

At the end of that same day, a man came in, asking if he could see me for just a moment. A friend of his had committed suicide. He did not know what to do or how to feel.

What all of these people had in common was the startling appearance of loss in their lives. Each had a choice. The loss could be seen as a sign of meaninglessness, or as an opportunity to create meaning. The response to that choice determines the quality, the dignity, and, to some extent, the happiness of our years on earth.

When we suffer a loss, people try to fix it for us. We cannot stand to see others who are not all right. I have seen people who have lost spouses be told, shortly after the funerals, of other people who are perfect for them. Because our own vulnerability is so frightening, we feel that if only we can fix it for someone else, we will be safer. The deep losses of life are not fixable, however, and the greater the loss, the more inappropriate the strategy of solution.

Those who are in trouble need a calmness of soul from those who care for them. We have to be able to look upon their distress and allow them to bear it. We can share their sadness; we cannot fix their pain. In the book of Job, when Job's friends first see him after the succession of tragedies that befall him, they sit on the ground beside him and weep. Their first reaction is admirable. Only later, when they try to explain to Job why this happened to him, are they condemned. What loss cries for is not to be fixed or to be explained, but to be shared and, eventually, to find its way to meaning.

When we experience a loss, a hole opens up inside of us. It is almost as if the loss itself plows right through us, leaving us gasping for air. We bleed through that opening, and sometimes old wounds are reopened. Things we thought were safely inside, patched over, healed, prove painful again in the wake of the new pain.

Very slowly, the immediate agony subsides. Around the edges of that opening, things begin to heal. Scar tissue forms. The hole remains, but instead of allowing only a constant stream of emptying, it begins to permit things to enter. We receive some of the love and wisdom that loss has to give us. Now is when loss can have content beyond the ache. This is the time to create meaning. Pay attention to what comes in that open space. Nothing can make the pain go away. Making loss meaningful is not making loss disappear. The loss endures, and time will not change that truth. But now it has some purpose.

In the Bible, God often speaks to Moses. There is only one time when a Divine communication is given directly to Moses' brother, Aaron: after the deaths of Aaron's sons. At first the communication seems paradoxical, but then it makes sense. Aaron is changed by this greatest tragedy. A part of him is opened, but through his pain he can hear something that until this moment was too muffled, too distant. Through loss, Aaron hears the voice of God.

To make loss meaningful requires courage. Courage is the ability to do what one believes is right, knowing that others may strongly and even persuasively disagree.

Early in my rabbinic education, I chose not to go to a congregation. While I loved teaching, I was not sure I could manage to be there for people in their times of need without nervously drawing boundaries around myself. The world of books seemed safer, easier. Sometimes I got quite involved in the lives of my students, but the commitment was limited. Eventually the students graduated. I returned to books and writing. For many years after I was ordained as a rabbi, I taught college and graduate students, first at the University of Judaism in Los Angeles, then at the Jewish Theological Seminary in New York.

A secondary result of my choosing to teach was that I became confused about my identity. Was I a rabbi, an author, a teacher? For me, the question was symbolized by my decision about wearing a *yarmulke,* a head covering. I would wear one when teaching, praying, or studying—that was clear. But the rest of the time I felt uncomfortable. I did not want the first thing people noticed about me to be the religious signifier I was wearing on my head.

When I decided to become the rabbi of Sinai Temple in Los Angeles, however, I came to realize that a rabbi is simply who I am. I could not hide it behind a change of dress. Despite my discomfort, I could not evade the path I had chosen for my life. I remembered a great truth that I had read years before in the writings of Thomas Merton: It is a foolish life which is lived in the minds of other human beings. Was I going to be someone different because the bank teller, or the flight attendant, or the cab driver did not like me? Did I really wish to live in disguise? Trivial as the example may seem, for me, courage became the resolution to wear a *yarmulke* all the time.

Freedom is a gift given to us by our willingness to be brave. If we are always fearful of the judgments of others, we are slaves.

Sometimes it is loss that frees us from this bondage to the biases of others. This freedom is a great gift. When we realize that what we hold valuable can be gone tomorrow, we hold other things—like people's offhand judgments—less dear.

When Eliana got cancer, I knew she could die. But I did not believe it. Not for a moment did I think her illness would be fatal. But I knew it was possible.

Through the time of her surgery and after, I concentrated on taking care of our daughter. Focusing on Samara was easier than focusing on Eliana. Samara had clear, measurable needs, and if I satisfied them, she would be fine. To focus on Eliana was to admit the possibility that she could die. If she was recovering from surgery, she needed help around the house. If she was recovering from cancer, she needed help in her heart. To take in the reality of her cancer would have meant having to take in the reality that it could recur. To acknowledge our loss was to know that we could lose again.

It was too painful for me to reckon with the loss. It was so improbable, at age thirty-one, that a healthy and beautiful young woman would have cancer inside of her. She suffered from an ailment we could not see, that she had not felt. I was there in many ways—I was helpful, solicitous. But in an essential way, I was not there.

During crises, we enter a sort of twilight zone, when nothing seems quite real. There is a separate, darkened time of loss. For an outsider, that experience is often hard to fathom. That is why so many well-meaning people urged Eliana to "get back on track" as soon as possible. I have heard people say to those who are suffering: Get back to the way things were before; do not get sidetracked; resume your normal life.

But together my wife and I learned that to go back is to return to the path that brought us to our loss. Instinctively, Eliana resisted those who were pushing her to return to the road that culminated in this crisis. She came to understand that she needed to change her life. The answer was not in return but in transformation.

The transformation was harder for me. To return to what was would be a way to deny the seriousness of her diagnosis. I wanted to deny it. If life resumed to what it had been before, then what we faced was not a crossroads but a mere bump on the highway.

Suddenly the wisdom that I preach to others evaporated. I wanted to "go back" because I was frightened. I pretended we had not suffered a real, heart-wrenching loss, because the implications were too great.

I had begun this book before Eliana's cancer. This fact urges the question: Are we sometimes led to a thing in life that we will need? Writing this book may have been the way I was intended to teach myself that standing outside the circle of loss is cowardice, and that those we love deserve our courage.

During the writing of this book, my wife again and again would share with me her thoughts, her ideas, her reflections on loss. She constantly said she wished I had more time to make this book better, to include more, to think more, to feel more. Perhaps what she really wanted was not that I put more of myself into the book, but that the book find its way more thoroughly into me.

When Eliana was diagnosed with cancer, her doctor told her something remarkable. She said she had never had a patient who survived cancer for any length of time who did not end up blessing the cancer.

The frightening thing about loss is what we do to ourselves to avoid it. We know we cannot live without losing, but this knowledge does not prevent us from seeking to protect ourselves. So we narrow our souls. We draw ourselves tighter and tighter. No longer open to the world with all its hurts, we feel safe.

By narrowing ourselves, though, we end up more hurt than if we were free. For each time we protect ourselves, we make more and more frequent the things that could hurt us. As we draw the circle smaller, we increase all the space outside the circle, the space of things that cause us pain. So the recluse in a room is in more pain than the one who lives among other people, but the recluse is in pain *and* in prison. A friend once told me that he was willing to live with pain but not with suffering. In other words, he would bear the aches that life had in store, but he would not ruin life's richness with dread about the inevitable pain. He would live with open arms, knowing he could with-stand the hurt, indeed, that he could grow from it.

"Living takes courage, and courage takes faith" is perhaps the single inescapable truism that all searchers come to sooner or later. We cannot live without being prepared for loss. And we cannot face loss without knowing that we can survive it and make it meaningful.

My father is retiring from the rabbinate. He has been a prac-ticing rabbi for forty-five years. In his sermon on the High Holidays, as my father was summing up the motivation and story of his life, one scene kept repeating itself in his memory. He said:

> *I am a youngster, and I am sitting on a large windowsill in my mother's and my apartment. It is high on the third floor of the family home, and, as I sit there, I can look above the surrounding roofs toward the south of Boston. There, in clear reflection, is Dorchester Bay. For you see, our apartment was part of a building that had been built by a clipper-ship captain, and it was from the vantage point of where our apartment stood that his wife would place a telescope and look out to Dorchester Bay for the return of her husband and his ship. It was called the widow's walk. There was no telescope for my mother, as her husband would never return.*

My father's loss of his father was the defining moment of his life. But he transmuted that moment into meaning. It drove him and defined him. The loss never ceased to sting. Indeed, it is the pain that spurs us to make the loss matter.

The late Rabbi Shlomo Carlebach used to tell a story. Rabbi

Carlebach used to travel all through the world to give concerts of religious music, pray, play, and inspire people. Once he visited a small town in Eastern Europe, after the collapse of the Soviet Union. Unlike most people he met, the people of this town wanted nothing to do with him. They were cold, distant—they closed the door, literally and metaphorically, in his face. All except for one man.

In the town, Carlebach found one man who was loving, open, accepting. He spent some time with the man, and before he was about to leave the town, Rabbi Carlebach asked him the question that had been burning inside.

"There is something I need to know," said Rabbi Carlebach. "I understand the people of this town. I realize why they want nothing to do with a singing rabbi from the West. After all, they were devastated by the Holocaust. Then they lived for close to fifty years under the jackboot of Communism. I understand their anger. What I don't understand is you! Why are you so loving, why are you so . . . different?"

The man smiled. "I know why, and I can tell you when it happened. I am an old man, and I have lived in this town my entire life. And I recall one night before the First World War, a rumor swept through the town that there would be a pogrom. We were told that the Cossacks were coming, and they would loot and pillage and steal and destroy. So all the parents from the whole town gathered up all the children and brought us to the rabbi's house.

"It was the dead of winter. Scattered throughout the rabbi's house were all the children of the village, sleeping on his floor, in the kitchen, the living room, the study. The rabbi paced up and down all night looking out over the children as we slept. I was curled up in a small corner of the rabbi's study. He thought I was sleeping, but it was bitter cold—I could not sleep. He came up behind me and slipped his cloak off his shoulders, and he laid it over me and said, 'Good child, sweet child.'

"You know," said the man to Rabbi Carlebach, "it has been seventy-five years since the rabbi spread his coat on me—but it still keeps me warm."

In the midst of loss, in the cold night, with the threat of destruction hanging over everyone's head, the rabbi made a gesture of love. For the rest of that child's life, he was different, because he knew that fear and pain and even loss were not all. Because he knew that we cannot escape losing but we can help one another keep warm.

My deepest prayer to God used to be to spare me from the pains of life that I so dreaded. Now I see that that is the prayer of a child. As a man I do not pray for a life without pain. Instead I pray: "Dear God, I know that there will be pain in my life, and sadness, and loss. Please give me the strength to create a life, together with those whom I love, where loss will not be empty, where pain will not be purposeless. Help me find the faith to make loss matter. Amen."

Two

_____

Home

A home is something that you lose.
—A Holocaust survivor

wo years ago, I was invited to address a conference that took place in the synagogue in Harrisburg, Pennsylvania, where I grew up. I had been back twice before. Each time it seemed that I was stepping into the past. My family had moved from Harrisburg when I was ten years old. Now I drove through the streets not as an adult, but as a child. With the eyes of a child, I saw the homes where my friends used to live, the river my brothers and I walked along, the modest four-lane street we thought was the greatest thoroughfare in the world.

The overnight flight landed early in the morning, and so I arrived at the synagogue an hour before my talk was scheduled. At the invitation of the organizers, I wandered the building, looking for a quiet spot to review my notes and collect my memories. I found myself in the small chapel, alone.

Although I had previously returned to the synagogue, I had not been in that chapel for almost thirty years. It looked the same.

When I sat down, I remembered Mr. Weiss.

Mr. Weiss led the children's services. Each week as the parents went to the main service, they would drop off all the kids at the chapel for prayers with Mr. Weiss. He was an old man, a Holocaust survivor, with an Eastern European accent and a gentle face. Mr. Weiss had no charisma, but he was kind. The children loved him. I loved him. Week after week, Mr. Weiss would assign us parts in the service, encourage us, guide us through. When someone did a particularly nice job, Mr. Weiss always had a reward handy. He would sneak a Luden's cherry cough drop into our hands.

I treasured those cough drops. They were small red jewels, a sign that I had done well, that Mr. Weiss approved.

Now, as I sat in that same chapel, Mr. Weiss came back to me. Though I had not thought about him in years, he was newly vivid in my imagination, his hand on my back, helping me through the prayers. Why had Mr. Weiss been so important to me? When Mr. Weiss was pleased, I believed God was pleased as well. We were children at prayer, looking for favor. Mr. Weiss was God's representative. The cough drops seemed to fall from heaven.

That small chapel was an untroubled place to me when I was a child. Mr. Weiss knew God, and we knew Mr. Weiss. Through him, each of us prayed as we were supposed to, and believed what we were taught.

Decades had passed. I was overcome with sadness. Mr. Weiss had died years ago. I was no longer a child. I was hardly as sure as I once had been of God's blessing, or of God. Everything in that chapel whispered loss.

We have homes in our lives, one after the other, and one after
the other we lose them. That chapel was not where I lived, but
it was a spiritual home. Like any childhood home, it could not
last. From the first human beings onward, from Adam and Eve
to us, we all end up outside of the garden. The day comes when
we have to make our gardens in memory; for me that chapel was
a precious place. But now Mr. Weiss lived in me through memories of those cough drops, slipped sweetly, secretly, into my
hand. I wished I could feel them still.

We spend our entire lives in search of home, for we must be
exiled to live. Pushed out of our first home when we are born,
each of us finds his way into a large and frightening world. The
newborn's cry is a symbol of the shocks that await. We will lose
a succession of homes in a lifetime. With each leaving, a piece
of ourselves stays behind. Home is not only the walls and the
fields, but the bit of our soul that rests, that finds peace in that
place.

I measure my life by the homes I have lived in—one from
birth to age six, another from ages six to ten, another (in a new
city) from ten to seventeen. Each one carries with it the sweetness and trouble of that time of life. All of them remind me of
the way loss works in our lives. Each place has a symbolic meaning in my memory.

The story of Eden is about the passage from the comfortable
home of youth to the larger, threatening world. The passage is

neither welcome nor easy. The first exile in the Bible parallels
the experience of our lives. Our small, snug homes do not
endure.

While in Eden, Adam and Eve do not realize they live in paradise, because they know nothing else. But they also do not
know themselves. Having lived only in the garden, they know
no pain, no yearning. It is struggle that leads to growth, and they
do not grow in the garden. They must face the "thorns and
brambles" of the world in order to grow. Today, as in the biblical tale, the loss of the garden is the beginning of knowledge.

Each person loses the garden at a different stage of life. Many
do not feel the loss of home until they actually, physically leave.
For years I taught freshmen in college. Most freshmen are away
from home for the first time. Even those who were most anxious
to leave and be on their own feel the loss keenly.

The loss that they feel is not only of a place but of a piece of
themselves. Leaving home is a farewell to childhood. The child
who was coddled or disciplined or loved a certain way at home
is unknown to contemporaries at school. Identities must be
established anew; the freshmen must make new homes, which
means they must remake themselves.

We are part of all the places we have been. When I returned
to that chapel, I became reacquainted with a piece of myself that
I left there. When new students would come to my office, they
knew that something in them was missing. Their footing was
unsure. The tentative knocks on my door were from people who
were not sure of the response they would get, because this place
was not home. Yet they also knew that something new was waiting to be discovered.

A parade of students uneasy in their new surroundings came to see me. One student was afraid of going back home, of slipping too easily into old patterns with her parents and siblings. School was the chance to re-create herself, and she did not like what she had been. She feared the gravitational force of her old home, that it would pull her down. At the same time, she missed its certainties. When I asked if she feared being pulled down by her family, she smiled, and said, "Yes. But I also have a fear of flying."

One student sat in my office once, a tall, handsome young man, with tears in his eyes. Barry had gotten a poor grade on his first test, and he had only one question: "How will I tell my parents?"

We talked several times that semester about leaving home. Everything he ever did was to connect himself to his parents, to his home, which was troubled. His parents did not have a good marriage, and they lived through him. When he did well in school, home was calm. When he did badly or disappointed expectations, things blew up in the house. Barry's fear was that if he did badly he would lose home, which was held together by his accomplishments.

Gradually, Barry concluded that the home he needed was not one that depended on his achievements. In a process that was very painful, he let go of the idealized home he believed in. He began to turn to others around him who cared for him when he did well and when he did not. Barry's self-regard grew through the belief that finding a place in this world is dependent not on his grade-point average but on the seriousness and sweetness of his soul.

By the end of the next year, Barry's parents had in fact divorced. They sold the home he had grown up in. But although Barry was saddened, he did not feel cast out. He had a home now, in the only place he could be sure would not disappear.

To leave home requires faith. In the most straitened circumstances, this faith is taken for granted. When refugees clamber onto boats in the hope of finding a better life, they must have faith that they will dock in a better place than the one they left behind. But even for that college student, to leave is an act of faith. Without loss we cannot grow. But without faith, we cannot bear to lose.

In the Bible, after Adam and Eve eat from the tree, they are condemned to death. Were they initially immortal, or always mortal? This question has been debated for centuries. My own view is that the Bible intended them to be mortal—for there were two trees in the garden: the tree of knowledge and the tree of life. Why, if they were not destined to die, would there be a tree of life? Yet *they were not conscious of their own mortality.* The secret of the garden is that Adam and Eve live as they do because they do not know they will die. God says, "As soon as you eat from the tree you shall die," though in fact they do not die, not right away. But they are aware of death, and that awareness can never be erased. Once Adam and Eve know that life is not forever, paradise is gone. They are exiled to face the perennial human challenge of making life full, knowing it is brief.

Curiously, at the beginning of the story, God forbids Adam and Eve to eat from the tree of knowledge but not from the tree of life. Why not the tree of life? Because Adam and Eve have no motivation to eat from it, since they do not realize that they will die. But once they have eaten from the tree of knowledge, they suddenly see their own bodies as fragile. They realize they will not live forever, and they become afraid. God must exile them because now they will seek out the tree of life. Now they hunger for eternity.

Their first reaction, after eating the fruit, is to dress themselves. Sexuality becomes critical not only because it reflects Adam and Eve's heightened awareness of themselves as bodies, but because through children we seek to perpetuate ourselves, to escape the enormity of death. To have children is to cheat death. After we are gone, we will still be here. Adam and Eve's first action, upon leaving the garden, is to conceive and bear children.

The garden represents a double exile. First is the exile from the security and innocence of childhood. When we are children, we do not know that things fade and break and die. We live with the illusion that nothing will change. One day that illusion is shattered, smashed by the truth that we cannot return to the garden of permanence. That is the primary exile, one from which we never recover. Much of what we accomplish in life stems from the recognition that our span is brief. We strive to make a mark. Eden means evermore.

The second exile is external. This time we are exiled not from our childhood innocence but from the physical space in which we live. Adam and Eve leave the garden. They cannot know what awaits them. The world "out there" is frightening and exciting. The same emotions that rise up from the pages of the Bible live inside each of us.

The loss of home is the loss of a place we have loved. The

love we feel for things makes us human, and the loss of them is what deepens this humanity within us.

Sitting in that chapel, I tried to remember myself as a child. What were my friends like? What did we care about; what did we know? I wanted, however briefly, to become that early version of myself. Adam and Eve wish to return to the garden not because of what the garden is, but because of who they were when they lived there. In the days of the garden they were innocent, without cares. Now they have knowledge and heartache.

Every loss in the world has a corresponding loss in our souls.

The whole world, taught Rabbi Nachman of Bratzlav, is a very narrow bridge, and the essence of life is not to be afraid. The world is a bridge on which we pass from one thing to another. There is no stability. Each new place, new change, creates fear. Rabbi Nachman did not compare the world to a field on which we might rest, but to a bridge, the symbol of passage, of journeying. And the secret is not to find a safe place, but to navigate the narrow crossing and remain unafraid.

I was living in Los Angeles in January of 1994, when it was struck by a powerful earthquake. During an earthquake, there is nowhere to hide. The ground beneath one's feet pitches like the deck of a ship, and one is betrayed by home.

My wife and I woke up at 4:31 A.M. feeling shaken like bugs in a bottle. There is a tremendous, roaring noise that accompanies an earthquake that sounds like a train rumbling through the living room. It takes but a moment to realize what is going on, since people who live in L.A. expect that eventually the "big one" will come. But the days and years that go by without a serious earthquake lull one back to calm. When the quake hits, it is a stunning surprise.

The world was dark, and we waited for light. Never have I been so grateful to see the sun come up. At least something was the same: The sun still rose in the morning. We walked outside to see our neighbors and reflect with wonder that we were still alive. We marveled over the huge hole torn up in the street. Then we realized that the freeway connection near our house, the one most of us drove on every morning, had collapsed. Turn 4:31 A.M. into 4:31 P.M., and everything would have looked different.

On the day following the earthquake, I went with some colleagues to check on the University of Judaism, where I taught. Glass was shattered all over the building. Pipes had burst, and water seeped through some of the floors. Part of the concrete façade of the building had fallen. The damage was arbitrary and awesome—it looked as though several small bombs had been dropped in select portions of the building, leaving some spots untouched and others devastated.

We walked into the dining hall, where part of the ceiling had collapsed. Pieces of it lay draped over tables, and a fine dust covered the rug. I stepped into my office. It was mostly intact, save some scattered books and papers, and a computer that had fallen, its monitor hanging from a chord wrapped around it like a noose.

There was a great deal of damage in the building, but nothing quite so affecting as in the library itself. Thousands of books had fallen from the shelves and were lying in great heaps on the floor. There were old books, holy books, prayer books. The impact spawned some improbable combinations. Next to a modern paperback novel was the medieval law code of Maimonides; lying on top of a mystical work on Jewish meditation was last week's *New Republic* magazine; liberals and traditionalists, old antagonists fell together; ancient and modern, fringe and mainstream, magazines, books, pamphlets—there was no discrimination in chaos.

To see a large building look as though it has been kicked over and over again by a giant is frightening. I felt a sickness deep in my stomach, not because of any danger—although the aftershocks were unsettling—but because my place in the world suddenly grew a little less secure. I felt as if I was standing on a high rooftop and had just learned that the railing was not perfectly sturdy. The world felt wobbly.

In the prayer services on Yom Kippur, there is a chilling line that recalls the devotions of the Temple: The High Priest would pray on behalf of the inhabitants of Sharon, whose city was subject to earthquakes, "May it be Your will O God and God of our Ancestors, that their houses not become their graves." The next day I learned that the students had poured out of the dormitories onto the basketball court at 4:40 in the morning, right after the earthquake struck, to recite this ancient prayer. And I remembered how this green and good earth can seem in a moment arbitrary and unkind. Suddenly and briefly, we were no longer at home. We were unwelcome visitors who had been told that our stay was at the kind sufferance of the host, and that the host was growing impatient.

I did fear during the earthquake. The date was fixed in my mind, January 17. But loss and blessing take on peculiar combinations in our lives. Three years later, on January 17, in the early morning, our daughter was born.

Our link with the earth is featured in the legend of Adne Sne, "man of the mountain." His form is exactly that of a human being, but he is fastened to the ground by means of an umbilical cord, upon which his life depends. Once the cord snaps, he will die. The legend expresses the profound reliance human beings have on the earth. Yet modern society has begun cutting away at that cord. Are we sure we can survive if we continue to sever the connection, to fray and gnaw at the cord each day? We use all our technology to remove ourselves from the natural world so that we can be safe. But the only perfect safety is death.

When I first moved to Los Angeles, one of my great surprises was the "car-pool lane." On the freeways, several sections are marked off for car pools. These lanes are supposed to encourage Angelinos to group together and so reduce the congestion on the roads. What surprised me is that a car pool is defined as two people. Growing up, I had always thought of a car pool as a bunch of people, but the signs were a reflection of a reality: We are increasingly isolated. Now, two people form a group! The danger, the annoyance, the inconvenience of other people is being gradually eliminated. Driving around L.A. and other cities, we usually see one person driving alone.

In the car we do connect, but to a voice on the radio. We become part of a community of people who never meet, who have no true dialogue. We feel included because we share opinions with nameless others. It is a pitiful parody of community, of the closeness that human beings were designed to share.

Recently I participated with other religious leaders in a panel discussion about the new millennium. One person spoke about how technology is tying us together. True, we can e-mail people on the other side of the globe. I can turn on my television and find out what is happening in Thailand or Turkey in a matter of moments. But is this "globalization" really tying us together?

Technology, quipped the Swiss writer Max Frisch, is the knack of so arranging the world that we do not have to experience it. Humanity has insulated itself from the world for good reason. Our homes keep out the cold. Roofs fend off the rain and snow. Boats and planes enable us to experience more of the globe than would otherwise be possible. Yet there is a corresponding cost, an offsetting loss.

I sit alone in my car. I get money from an automatic teller. I make contact with other people through a computer screen. Many people conduct business via phone and fax, e-mail and voice mail, instead of by traveling. Even letters, which are marked by the personality of the correspondent's handwriting, the choice of pen and ink, stationary and stamp, are losing out to the impersonal ephemera of e-mail.

Technology does not so much tie us together as its failure does. When technology breaks down, we encounter one another. When the earthquake hits, we pour onto the streets. When e-mail and voice mail are down, we must walk into one another's offices and speak face-to-face. When the electricity fails on a modern block of homes, people meet one another and talk. A blizzard does more for community than all the modems on earth.

But when power is restored, so is our seclusion, our technological exile. We reinforce our exiles by building fortress houses and staying there because our home "entertainment systems" can, along with food delivery, give us all we think we need.

Some of my younger congregants sit in their rooms night after night, talking to others through a keyboard. Their society is artificial, electronic. They speak to me about how isolated they feel. How deep can kinship be if it is projected through a computer screen?

When I was a teenager I used to sit in my room and read and play chess. Although I had friends, I spent a lot of time alone. My major social outlet was to talk on the phone. The phone is like the computer—it offers intimacy without danger. You can get close, but not too close.

Had I been a teenager in the time of computers, I don't know that I ever would have come out of that room. The computer is more seductive, more interesting than the phone. In adolescence, I was uncomfortable enough to feel safe in my room and unsafe elsewhere.

When we moved to our new house in Philadelphia, my three brothers and I had to choose bedrooms. We looked through the house. There was one bedroom on the third floor—all the others were on the second floor. I coveted that third-floor bedroom but was certain that one of my older brothers would claim it. To my amazement, neither did. They wanted to be on the second floor with everyone else. Only I craved the cocoon.

The third floor was removed from the world. The battle

between distance and closeness, a battle I have found myself in my whole life, was geographically joined in my own house. As I look back on it, my tools for isolation were pretty primitive. No computer, no answering machine, not even a television in my room. Maybe only that lack of diversion saved me from an even greater isolation. We can love aloneness too much.

Homes are made through attachment. Connection to others is the great generator of meaning in life. When we are without deep attachments, our lives skim along the surface. We take racing dives into life, never plunging to the depths, because we are not sure that anyone else will be there with us. Technology does not encourage these deep attachments. There is no real loss when someone signs off the chat room.

We must wander, we must escape the confinement of the womb and first home. Teenagers spend so much time on the phone for the reason that I did, because it keeps human contact safe. What does that behavior say of their parents, however, who do the same with e-mail? When we exile ourselves from the friction of dealing with others, we become what much modern technology pushes us toward—prickly, asocial, and self-obsessed people whose energies are absorbed by a screen and not by the alternately gracious and galling reality of other people.

First we must create real homes, which are built on real relationships. Then we must lose them. Exile is the prerequisite for growth. This idea is enshrined in the structure of the Western world's shared sacred book.

The Torah is the core of the Hebrew Bible. In the five books, the outline is clear: Humanity begins in Eden, in a perfect promised place that humanity loses. Paradise is gone, but not forgotten.

Yet there is a paradise that waits for humanity at the other end. The Bible culminates in a promised home. God will guide the Israelites through the desert so that they can inherit the land. The promise begins with Abraham and is reiterated in each generation. The promised land takes on a special character because the people are not born there. The Jewish people are born with Abraham, far away from the place that will be called Israel. They are born in exile, dreaming from the first of a land they have not seen.

In the final book of the Torah, the book of Deuteronomy, Moses glowingly describes the wonders of the new land. It will flow with milk and honey. It will be a perfect, lovely garden. In tropes that recall the garden of Eden, Moses urges his followers to build an ideal community, to realize their mission of becoming a "holy nation."

This well-plotted scenario—bookended with paradise on one end and the promised land on the other—has only one problem. When we reach the conclusion of the Torah, when the last verses of Deuteronomy are read, the Israelites are still in the wilderness. The Torah is a book without an ending.

The book of Joshua does describe the arrival of the Jewish people into Israel. But the book of Joshua is far less important, less read, less venerated than the initial five books. It is not included in the scroll of the Torah, perhaps because when the people do enter Israel, there is none of the promised perfection. Joshua is a book that chronicles struggle, difficult and often bloody struggle, to conquer the land. The counterpart to Eden, which has been promised, is nowhere to be found. The land does not flow with milk and honey.

Why does the Torah, which assured us for so long of a glorious entry into Israel, deprive us of the consummation we expect and desire?

We end in the wilderness because there is no perfect promised land—except as a promise. A promised land is ideal, untroubled. That does not exist in this world. A promised land is free of the strife that darkens and afflicts even the most serene life. Immigrants were told that America was the ideal land, that the streets were paved with gold. They came and found that the streets were lined with sweatshops. America proved to be a land of opportunity, which is a far more ambiguous and difficult gift than a land of gold-lined streets. Similarly, the Israelites had triumphs in their new home, but also catastrophes. They discovered that an idyllic home is a dream, for they live in the world, and the world is a wilderness.

There is no place in this world that is free of suffering, because exile touches everyone. Each year on Passover, Jews conclude the seder, the ritual meal, with the incantation "Next year in Jerusalem!" However, if the seder takes place in Jerusalem, the incantation is not "Next year here!" Rather, Jerusalemites conclude with "Next year in a *rebuilt* Jerusalem!" In other words, Jerusalem as it is promised, free of the political and social agony of the ages, free of the daily difficulties and tragedies of life, a Jerusalem where the milk and honey truly flow, where the glorious visions of the prophet obtain, where we are finally, truly home. Next year out of the wilderness.

We live in temporary homes as we travel through the wilderness. Nothing is permanent, and no place ideal. Our task is not to gather in the shade of the garden's trees, but to grow as we hold hands through the wilderness. The journey is made bearable, even wonderful, by community and by faith. There is an old joke about two men, Schwartz and Rosen, who are walking to synagogue. Someone stops them and asks Rosen, "Why are you going to synagogue? Schwartz, here, is a believer—I know why he is going. But you're not religious!" Rosen answers, "Well, Schwartz goes to talk to God, and I go to talk to Schwartz." Religion is built not only on the relationship to God but on the connection with one another. Walking with others embodies faith, makes it real, assures us that each step is worthwhile and that the dream of Eden need not disappear.

The remarkable point about the wilderness in the Bible is that escape appears possible. God bars Adam and Eve from reentering Eden. They can never return to the paradise from which they came. Yet God does not destroy the garden. Instead, God simply stations sentries and a spinning, fiery sword to guard it. The garden exists but is inaccessible. Similarly, the Israelites wander for forty years, but the journey could have been completed in far less time. They come within months, perhaps even weeks, of entering the land in that time. We envision the end. The garden, the promised land, seems ever close. We can imagine a world better than our own. Paradise is not beyond our imagination; it is merely beyond our grasp.

We live, each of us, as a child of wilderness. We are enmeshed in loss, in search of home.

Home may not be where you grew up. It may not be the parlor where you shook off snow boots or watched TV. Home may be a place unseen but vividly imagined.

There was a time of fields, friends, of hot chocolate on winter nights and fresh new birthday toys that thrilled us with a
wonder scarcely felt anymore. Even if we still live in the same
house, that home is gone, pushed out by the inevitability of
aging. A nation loses a historical home, becomes the victim of
violent forces in the world. The individual's loss is more grad-
ual, more predictable, more internal. Yet each shares the sad,
sudden truth that what we loved is gone. The only true paradises
are those we have lost.

Sometimes I think home for me is on a bridge that passes over
a lake that was behind my house when I was a small child. My
brother and I would go there almost every day. The bridge had
none of the accoutrements of home except that it felt like it was
mine, and I belonged there. That bridge still stands, but it is no
longer mine. Even though the lake has remained unchanged, the
boy has not. You can't go home again not because home is no
longer the same but because you are no longer the same. Home
may be static, but people change. Exile is a series of circles that
originates in the ever-shifting self. When I stood on that bridge
again, there was some kernel of the little boy in me, the boy who
thought of that lake and that bridge as the hub of the world, the
boy who saw the swans on the lake so often he gave them names.
But the kernel was overlaid with too much other experience of
the world to return undivided to that place. If that was home for
me, I am left without one in that deep sense.

In *All Quiet on the Western Front*, the soldier returns home on
leave: "There is my mother, there is my sister, there my case of
butterflies, and there is the mahogany piano—but I am not
myself there. There is a distance, a veil between us."

The veil is the spinning sword of Eden, and we cannot pass it by.

The exiles we endure are partly of our own choosing and partly the caprices of life. We leave, give up, turn our backs on worlds we later remember with regret. As I complete this book, I have just turned forty. Since I was seventeen I have lived in sixteen different places, never for more than two years at a time. Each time I left, I wondered what I was leaving behind. We are like trails of light, and bits of us remain where we have been, while other parts streak off to elsewhere. Sometimes what we leave behind is what we should have taken, but who is granted this foreknowledge?

We rarely know for sure exactly what the leaving will mean, or whether and how we might return. Who knew that this path, this tree, this crumbled wall would prove so dear in memory? Another world created and destroyed, often by our own choice. Necessity and hope have driven us to make a different place. Out of those fragments of memory we create art. Some of the greatest literature of both ancient and modern times was written by those in exile. For most of us, what we create from our fragments is our understanding of each new place and the patterns of the world. I see each new place I live in with the eyes that have seen other places. This couch connects to that one in memory. What is before us always bears traces of what we have left behind. Each new love stirs a remembrance of the old.

In the Bible, the career of Abraham begins with God's saying
"Go forth" (Gen. 12:1). An alternate translation of the Hebrew
phrase is "Go to yourself." Only through leaving can Abraham
learn his true character.

Abraham left because he had faith. He knew the world was
wide and dangerous. Inside of him, however, was a compass of
faith. He knew that the compass might not always point him in
an ideal direction, but wherever it sent him, he could make
meaning from the experiences that would befall him.

A marvelous feature of the story is that the phrase "Go forth"
appears one more time in Abraham's life. Indeed, it occurs only
twice in the Bible, both times in connection with Abraham. In
the last major episode of Abraham's life, the binding of Isaac,
God tells Abraham again, "Go forth." He is now an old man,
with a lifetime's worth of experiences, disappointments, and triumphs. Yet he is still a wanderer.

Abraham has lost many homes, but he has never really been
homeless. He has carried his home inside of him, because he has
lived with faith. Abraham knows that he is not alone.

A strange custom developed among Eastern European pietists
in the last few hundred years. Jews took upon themselves the full
weight of exile voluntarily. The practice of voluntary exile—
oprikhtn goles—was designed to humble one and remind him that
everything comes from God, that possessions are an illusion,
and that true faith will leave one's well-being in the Divine's
hands. Self-imposed exile was penance for sins real or imagined.
The penitent left home with nothing, resolved to live as a beggar. It was a way of reenacting the punishment of the biblical

Cain: to be a wanderer on the earth, at the mercy of not only the elements but the kindness or cruelty of other human beings.

One would wander, with no fixed destination, often for no fixed amount of time. Life would happen; chance (or God's design) would determine the fate of the wanderer. Sleeping in the cold street or the woods, living on scraps of food at times, the exile would expose himself to whatever living without a home meant. The wandering also expressed a deep restlessness of soul. It enabled the world, with all its harshness and unpredictability, to work upon the soul of the wanderer, to make it humble, pliant, open to God. By ripping away the stability of home, the wanderer hoped to uncover the tenderness of heart necessary to reach spiritual heights.

Each individual loses his or her place in the world. At the end of her life, my grandmother spoke for the first time about the home she had left in Russia as a young child. She had been four or five when her family picked up and left, and only now, in her seventies, was she speaking of it to her grandchildren. Though she had lived her entire life after coming to America in Boston, though she had a Boston accent and rooted passionately for the Red Sox, all of a sudden I felt that she never stopped missing that dimly remembered estate in Russia from which she came.

Yet we make the loss of homes in the world meaningful by building them inside of our own souls. We build by taking from a place the lessons it has to teach. The more systematically and thoughtfully we can do so, the more each place can be our teacher. As adults, keeping a journal is one way to reflect on where we have been. Keeping in touch with those who have shared our past is another. A third way is by journeying back, in memory, from time to time to see how the past looks with the wisdom of intervening years. Each year my childhood looks a little different to me, because I understand things in a way I did not before.

Each place we leave is a room in the home we build inside. The mortar is the belief that each home was necessary to make us who we are. We should not dread leaving or tremble at the unknown places where we have to go. We are wanderers all, children of the wilderness.

Life is a bridge, and we should not be afraid.

Loss contains within it the potential for meaning. Anna Freud, in her work with children who had suffered terrible traumas, described an orphaned child after the blitz bombing of London who kept mumbling, "I am nobody's nothing." In that terrible phrase is the bottom of loss. The child felt she belonged nowhere. But she also gave the critical clue to what she needed in order to climb out of the abyss.

The severed link is reconnected by love and by faith. When I visit people in hospitals, their first declaration is often that they want to go home. Home represents the world away from sickness. Without the usual surroundings, in a hospital gown, in an unfamiliar place, they feel less important, less central to the lives of others. Visitors, prayers, assurances of love can change this feeling dramatically. People still want to go home, but not because they fear being forgotten. Home is not the only safe place anymore, because home is less a place in the world than a place inside.

The opposite of exile is redemption. Exile is the loss of home, and redemption is the finding of a home, a real home. Redemption is a product of the love of others, of our own strength, of memory, and of faith. Together these factors combine to make real the prayers of the exile, that he might one day be truly at peace, really at home.

The faith that creates a home is the faith we have in our ability to generate a worthy place. As the seed contains the fruit, taught the Gerer Rebbe, so exile contains the essence of redemption within itself. If we can love, if we can believe in the possibility of figuring out a place for ourselves in this world, we can endure losing home. For we will create a new one.

In ancient Greece, it was claimed that the name Homer comes from *homeras*, the Greek word for hostage. According to legend, Homer was so called because he was a wanderer, driven out of each community in which he sought to live. Homer's own name offers an insight into his portrait of Odysseus, a wanderer who always seeks home.

Still the word "hostage" reminds us of a paradox: that the external condition does not create freedom. The vagabond, who has no place to rest, may be spiritually hostage, or spiritually free. Cain laments in the Bible that his punishment—to be forever wandering—is too great for him to bear. The whole world is at his feet, but his complaint is that of the prisoner behind bars. The world is more spacious than Eden, but he feels like a prisoner in a large cage. In contrast, Adam and Eve, before they ate the fruit, lived in a small garden but were free. Space alone does not make liberty, nor lack of space a prison. Freedom consists of the possibility of meaningful action in a setting that allows self-determination.

This struggle for physical freedom is what drives the exile to seek internal freedom. When the world does not permit movement, even then one's own soul can take flight. We know from history that some of the most beautiful meditations of humanity have been written by those imprisoned or enslaved: from Epictetus to Boethius to Anne Frank. When the body is in fetters, the soul seeks to burst free.

Rabbi Aryeh Levin was called the holy man of Jerusalem. He spent his adult life in Israel, visiting prisoners—many of them political prisoners—and bringing them comfort, food, and spiritual sustenance. Once, after Passover, some of the Jewish prisoners told Rabbi Levin that the Passover seder was good but that something important was missing. Because they were in prison, they could not perform the traditional rite of opening the door for Elijah. That act in the seder is what invites redemption, for Elijah is the herald of the Messiah. Surely there is no enslavement more absolute than the inability to coax forth redemption.

Rabbi Aryeh's response was: "Every man is in a prison of his own self. He cannot leave by going out of the house, but only through the door of the heart. And to make an opening for himself in his own heart—that anyone can do, even a prisoner behind bars. And then he truly will be spiritually free."

The insistence that all human beings can make their way through the heart is born partly of the exilic experience. And it began as early as did humanity.

How do we keep faith, hope, spirit in exile? The question begins as a sociological one, but it becomes personal. No human being on earth is home. We are criss-crossed exiles from the possibility of permanence, from our own geographic homes, from places and people we love, from ourselves.

Our spirit is sustained by the love of others. To be cast out is to lose trust, but to build a home inside is to regain that trust in ourselves and in other people. Children who move from foster home to foster home have no faith in the world. But the stability and love of a true home often can reverse their wariness. I have known many people who grew up in homes filled with anger or discontent who nonetheless went on to build homes filled with warmth and peace. The basis of the change was the certainty that leaving can be an opportunity. We crave the stability of one place, and the place is built not on land but on community, trust, and love.

We know that losing a home is often the spur to achievement. Had they not left the garden, Adam and Eve would have remained static, silent. The world would not have unfurled for their descendants. Careful readers of the story notice that there is no typical day in Eden. What Adam and Eve might have done in paradise is not described, or even mentioned. For nothing can happen in perfection. Perfection is static. Wandering is dynamic. Loss is real.

Losing our homes in the world is creative. Making them inside ourselves is healing. Mr. Weiss and his cough drops are gone. They do touch my life, however, recaptured by the experience of going back to the home I have lost.

On the evening of my installation as the rabbi of Temple Sinai, I spoke about Mr. Weiss. I told the congregation of my memories. Even though I stood in a sanctuary that seated 1,000 people, to me it was a cozy home, a home I had somehow recaptured.

The next morning as I came in for work, boxes of Luden's cherry cough drops covered my desk.

The Chofetz Chaim was a great rabbi whose fame spread worldwide in the nineteenth and twentieth centuries. Once he was once visited by a group of American tourists. They found him alone in his study, with nothing but a rickety writing table and a few books. "Where are all your possessions?" they asked him in surprise. The Chofetz Chaim smiled, and asked, "Where are yours?" They explained that they were without possessions, they were just passing through. The Chofetz Chaim nodded. "So am I." At a spiritual level, the knowledge that we are strangers grants us some peace. We reach above the anxiety of our alienness, and it becomes a certainty of life.

Three

Dreams

The eye has a dark part and a light part.
One can see only through the dark part.
—Tanhuma, Tetzave

Next—David . . ."

"David" was never followed by my last name. Each time my excitement grew, only to be quashed. In the group of some 200 children, it seemed that there were more than the usual number of Davids, and they all made it. Not me.

I was ten years old. We lived down the block from a Little League field. I used to go each day to watch the older kids play, and dream about playing there, too. This was the first year—and since we moved the following year to another city, also the last—that I was eligible to play. Along with my friends, I tried out for the team after having practiced all summer. As I recall, during the tryouts I showed a somewhat less than thorough grasp of the game by sliding into first base.

My oldest brother accompanied me on the fateful day when they would read the names of the children who had made the league. One by one they read through the team lists, my breath catching with each new name, praying it might be mine. I would sit on the bench all season, happily, I told myself, if only I had a uniform, if only I was part of the game. When the list was complete and I wasn't on it, I cried well into the night.

The dashing of an early dream is no less painful than the dashing of dreams we cherish later in life. Indeed, sometimes it is more painful, because children do not yet know that time heals. When children feel something, they believe it is forever.

Although my passion has long since waned, I was a sports fanatic growing up. I covered my walls with pictures of sports heroes, wrote players for autographs, memorized statistics. I spent hours dribbling basketballs, throwing footballs, swinging bats. Going to my first live baseball game when I was six years old was like a sacred pilgrimage. I dreamed of playing major-league baseball.

I will never play major-league baseball. Of course, I never could have. But there was a moment when it became clear to me that the dream was dead. At the age of twenty-five, I realized it would never happen, could never happen. Already many of the better ballplayers were younger than I. I felt a palpable loss. Before that day, the hope was as remote as could be, even practically impossible, but not so impossible that the fantasy did not still strike me in idle moments. The day I realized not only that I did not come close to having the talent—but that I was already *too old*—something that I had built inside me collapsed. Reality stole the fantasy for good. Perhaps the dream had always been absurd, but that didn't lessen my disappointment.

We live lives of successively shed hopes. Even the most accomplished person lives with the disappointment of unrealized dreams. I was once told by a thoughtful man who had been extremely successful, wealthy, and well-known, who had lived a life of variety and interest, "You know, I have had more failures than successes, and I've fulfilled fewer dreams than I've lost."

As a small child I wanted to be all sorts of things—a super-hero, a cowboy, a writer, a detective, an adult. There was no way of sorting dreams because the world had not yet closed its doors. Each new dream was the final one; today's choice was what I really wanted. But dreams shifted because they were not based on a knowledge of who I really was and because they involved no responsibility. As we get older and our dreams demand care, we handle them more tenderly. Now they are dreams whose realizations require that we change our lives. Now they are dreams whose losses can wound.

Faith asks us questions about our dreams: Are they worthy? Have we simply mused upon them in listless moments, or have we done something to ensure they come true? And the question that really tests us is whether or not—as we see life whittle away our dreams, dash them, and reshape them—we simply stop dreaming. Do we cut the cloth of our dreams to fit the frame of reality? Do we lose the parts of our dreams that rely on faith?

When we are young, we all build castles in the air. After all, as Thoreau once said, that is where castles should be, so long as we are prepared to put foundations beneath them. Now that we are older, have we stopped building? There was a time when our castles were so complete; we had planned our lives in detail, the moat was scooped out, the drawbridge envisioned, the spires and towers massive and lovely. Is it all gone?

Perhaps we do not lose our dreams because of thwarted base-ball careers, but what of life's blows that are far more vicious than losing out on Little League? My wife and I once lived down the hall from a couple who had given birth to a baby with a severe genetic disease. When we moved in, the child was nearly five years old, having lived longer than the norm. During the time we lived there, the boy died.

His parents faced his death courageously. They had been expecting it from the time he was diagnosed as an infant. There was great sadness, but the sadness was not only for his death but for the whole tragic trajectory of his life. He had been a sweet boy, but there was so little he could do or understand. His parents groped to find meaning in his life and death, and even set up a charitable foundation in his memory.

Toward the end of our stay in that building, our daughter was born. Eliana and I brought her home from the hospital, bursting with dreams. Everyone was healthy and very happy. Our friend from down the hall stopped by to see the baby. She saw my wife nursing our newborn, sitting next to a window overlooking the crisp winter day. She was truly happy for us, but also deeply sad about what she had endured.

"You know," she told my wife, "I signed up for what you got."

How do we keep faith when dreams that matter go awry?

Hope deferred makes the heart sick, teaches Proverbs 13:12. But dreams, like hopes, are not only deferred. Sometimes they are crushed. Then what becomes of the heart?

Once we cross over the boundary of childhood, dreams change. Perhaps the greatest illusion of youth, next to the stability of the world, is the constancy of dreams. We believe that the desire for this career or that vision of life will always stay.

Even those who believe they will never get what they want believe they will never change what they want.

Each year when I speak to high school students, I ask what they want out of life. I ask them if they believe their desires will change. Many of them say yes, but when I press them I realize their answers come from the wisdom of their heads—they have been told their dreams will change—but not of their hearts. "I can't believe I will ever *not* want to be a sportscaster," I was told several years ago by a young man who is now a doctor. I was his counselor, and he would sit on the sidelines at sports events in camp and call the games, even if no one was listening. "Sammy is rounding third!" When I heard he was entering medical school, I could not help imagining him announcing operations: "Herb is making the incision! And it's good!" Someday I will ask him if he changed his dream or if in quiet moments he still imagines his voice calling out over the crowd. Desires shift, sometimes abruptly, often with the steady, enveloping roll of a mist over a once-familiar landscape. Suddenly what was wished for is gone, and in its place lies another vista of the possible—another dream.

If the mists shift often enough, one no longer knows which vision to trust. That is why the epithet "dreamer" can be flattering or insulting. Dreams can be stimulants that propel a life. Repeated too often, unfulfilled, or unrealistic, they can also be the intoxicants that shield one from living.

In the final days of his life, the patriarch Jacob comes face-to-face with Pharaoh, the ruler of Egypt. Dispensing with the diplomatic niceties usually appropriate to such an occasion,

Pharaoh greets Jacob by asking, "How old are you?" (Gen. 47:8) Commentators assume that Pharaoh asks this question because he is astonished at Jacob's appearance. The toll of Jacob's misadventures is so great that his extraordinary journey can be read in the lines of his face. Before Pharaoh stands not the youthful dreamer but the pained and aged face of one whose wisdom has been wrung from anguish.

Jacob replies, "The years of my sojourn [on earth are] one hundred and thirty. Few and bitter have been the years of my life" (Gen. 47:9).

Instead of answering about his age, Jacob complains about the course of his life. Why does Jacob think of his years as few and bitter? He has suffered great losses, it is true—of his beloved wife Rachel, and for a long while his treasured son Joseph. Yet he has also accumulated vast wealth, built a large and ultimately reunited family, and helped in the birth of a great nation. Losses in life are inevitable. But few lives are so rich with accomplishment. What draws Jacob to so dour an assessment of his life? Jacob is devastated not because he is measuring his life against the lives of others, but because he is measuring life against his early dreams. Those first dreams of ease, of vigor, of safety resolved into a life of struggle. Jacob cannot forget what he had dreamed.

Lives that are measured against dreams seem slack and pale. The wonder that filled the heart of the youth from the day he fled home was betrayed by the reality of the world. To measure life by dreams is to ensure a residue of bitterness. Jacob thinks his life is bitter because it has been lived not in dreams but in the hardscrabble reality of the world.

When Jacob is a young man, he deceives his old, blind father and steals his older brother's birthright. Jacob flees because his brother Esau swears that upon the death of their father, Esau will kill him.

Jacob is a smooth and dissolute young man. He is a trickster, a con man. But he is also special—Jacob dreams. He has the magical wheel inside him that throws sparks out into the dusty streets of his tribal world.

Abraham went forth (*lekh l'cha*), but Jacob leaves (*va-yetze*). He is impelled not only by his deception but because he needs a bigger stage for his dreams. Every great dream begins with a departure. One must leave the physical or psychic setting of one's youth. Breaking with what was characterizes great dreams. The exile we spoke about earlier is the catalyst, and sometimes it is voluntary. The dreamer puts himself apart. He is the one who imagines different and wondrous enterprises. By that very act of imagination, he has left. He will return bearing something new.

Jacob finds himself alone for the first time. He places his head upon a stone and lies down to sleep. He dreams of angels who ascend and descend the ladder to heaven. Jacob's ladder originates in his special vision and his frightened heart. Though he gained the birthright, he lost his home, the connection to his parents, and whatever affection existed between himself and his brother Esau. The dream of the ladder is a gift of his loss.

Dreams of youth are golden. They have the haze of a pliable world, one that can be molded by our talent and effort. The range of obstacles, the weariness of years, the truth that our gifts may have a shorter stretch than we imagine—all of this does not seem real. The child may hate his or her world, but there will be a place to dream of a new one, where whims and narrowness will not reign, where crabbed streets will open into immense vistas, and as far as one can see, there will be nothing but green stalks of possibility.

Life, as Kierkegaard said, is lived forward but understood backward. The same is true of dreams. Jacob's dream of the ladder is the only uninterpreted dream in the Bible—perhaps because until we see the progress of Jacob's life, we cannot understand it.

Jacob arises, shaken but unchanged. His first reaction is to utter a memorable line: "Surely there is a God in this place and I did not know it" (Gen. 28:16). We might be lead to expect a different Jacob. Perhaps the dream has touched his heart and persuaded him to renew the painstaking work of honestly realizing his dreams. Instead, Jacob strikes a deal with God: "Jacob then made a vow, saying, 'If God remains with me, if He protects me on this journey that I am making, and gives me bread to eat, and clothing to wear—and if I return safe to my father's house—the Lord shall be my God'" (Gen. 28:20–21). Jacob wants his dreams fulfilled, now—and not by his own effort.

Having run away from home, living without his parents and their protection, Jacob has already lost too much. He is not prepared to risk further loss at the hands of a God who may make demands without offering returns. Jacob's is the psychology of entitlement. He believes himself special; he trusts the superiority of his own gifts.

Jacob has a certain trust in God as the guarantor of his dreams. There is a lovely story about Rabbi Shneur Zalman, who was once playing with his grandson, who himself was to become a renowned leader. The rabbi said to his small grandson, "Where is Zeide (Grandpa)?" The boy pointed to his grandfather's nose. "No, that is Zeide's nose. Where is Zeide?" The boy pointed to his beard, to his chest, and got the same answer. Finally, the boy climbed off his grandfather's lap and went into the next room. "Zeide!" he called. Rabbi Shneur Zalman walked in. "There is Zeide!" the boy cried triumphantly. For the child, Zeide is the one who comes when he is called. Jacob bases his dream on the same certainty about God. He may not know exactly what God is, but he is certain of one thing—God will be there when called.

Jacob does not yet realize the meaning of his dream. Unlike angels, he cannot fly. The ladders are real for him, but he must seek to climb them one by one, rung by rung.

When I was in high school, I brought home an English paper that had gotten a good grade but was filled with small mistakes. I was proud of the effort, because the teacher had praised the creativity even while noting the many errors. I showed it to my father, whose reaction I shall never forget. "David," he said, "you will never be a great chess player."

I could not imagine what he meant. I was indignant. First of all, I was making good progress in chess at the time. Second, my father knew nothing about the game whatsoever. Third, what did that have to do with the paper, of which I was proud? I asked him what he could possibly mean, and he gave me a valuable life lesson.

"I know almost nothing about chess. I know that you love it, just as you love writing." That was certainly true, and I admitted it. "Even though I don't know much about chess, I am sure," he continued, "that there are parts of chess that challenge your creativity and your invention. But I am also sure that there are parts of chess that require a careful attention to detail. I have no doubt that there are parts of the game you should study that are dull and repetitious. And I bet you ignore those parts because they don't grab you. The same pattern I see in your English papers runs through your work. You will never excel at anything—not writing, not chess—unless you overcome it. Every field will have its drudgery and its detail. You have to care about that, too."

He was exactly right. In chess, the endgame requires tremendous patience and attention to detail. I would ignore it in favor of the middle of the game, when the board is full of pieces and the fighting is intense and dramatic. The endgame is the grammar of the board—you can't speak chess well without it. Everything, from chess to life, has this same paradox, that the realization of dreams is found in daily acts of attention. Attention and effort are indispensable, but they are not sufficient. Mastery must be lightened by spontaneity.

Jacob is certain that life can be tamed. He does not yet realize the tremendous work and attention that are indispensable to meaningful living. He also assumes that he can figure out life— that it will not simply happen but that he can control it. I meet with this illusion again and again. A young man in my office asks me why the woman he is about to marry has qualities that are so different from the ones on his checklist. He was sure he could anticipate what he would need and what he would want. I try to explain to him that qualities do not exist in the air—they exist in people. You cannot simply ask for intelligence or charm; there are as many different kinds of intelligence and charm as there are people. You are not putting together a business deal, I hear myself telling him (with perhaps a bit more edge in my voice than is warranted), you are trying to understand a human being.

People confound. That is why you do not possess another, you love her.

Acceptance of the unpredictability of life, the loss of the illusion of control, is a crucial mark of maturity. People who have lived without controls, an unpredictable home, or explosive internal emotions often give themselves to the seductive dream of managing life according to plan. But for every way of doing something right, the possibilities of error, accident, or simple contingency are infinite. Life refuses to be broken and tamed.

That insight must come to Jacob over time. His dreams are ethereal blueprints, spun with threads of cloud. None of them will be realized without the effort and affliction that reality demands. Jacob is a golden boy. He has tricked others and gotten what was not his, the birthright. Now he will be tricked in turn.

Jacob has to work for seven years to marry Rachel, the girl he loves, only to be fooled at the last moment into marrying Leah. Still he persists, and after fourteen years, married to both Rachel and Leah, he leaves the house of his cousin Laban a wealthy man, with a large family and a secure future.

Jacob begins to understand that the central rule of life is that little is won without work. Even God does not grant the way one would wish. Jacob's dream of ease is shattered by the realities of life. Jacob's sense of grievance with the world is that it will not let him simply fly up the ladder.

Jacob has just begun to learn this lesson when he hears frightening news. His brother Esau is coming for him, accompanied by 400 men. For the first time, the dreamer knows dread. Jacob's original dream of a gentle, supportive world has been upended. He has come upon the trickery of Laban, who deceived him into marrying Leah when Jacob wished to marry Rachel. He has

been forced to work an additional seven years to marry the
woman he loves. Finally, he has progressed through genuine
toil, the conflicts and pain that love arouses, which is a require-
ment for making one's way in this world. Now he must face the
prospect of his own death.

Jacob sees his family safely across the river and then steps
back and is left alone in the camp. "And Jacob was left alone.
And a man wrestled with Jacob until the coming of dawn" (Gen.
32:24). Those two lines open a world of possibility. Who was
the man? Was it, as traditional commentators have often con-
tended, an angel? Or was it, as more modern psychologically
oriented interpreters argue, Jacob himself? With whom do we
wrestle when we wrestle alone?

The wrestling proceeds all night, and Jacob arises wounded.
He walks with a limp for the remainder of his days. One of the
greatest losses of youth has been inflicted upon him, the loss of
perfect bodily vigor. How much is lost on that fateful day when
we wake up and our leg or our back or our belly has betrayed
us? It is a loss of health and a loss of will—for "we" (the somatic
self) can no longer respond to "ourselves" (the conscious wish).
We are split and wounded.

Here is Jacob's second loss: He no longer can dream of ease.
When we are young, if granted health, we imagine the bodies
we will have. We wish to grow up beautiful and strong. When
Jacob rose up years before from that rock on which he dreamed,
he never imagined that he would have to grip the rock to steady
himself, to rise slowly, to feel unsure.

Few dreams are so cruelly upended as the dream of health, of
vigor. For almost fifteen years I have watched my mother struggle with her body. At the age of fifty-two, she suffered a stroke

that robbed her of her speech. Her right hand became useless. She walks with a limp. After years of therapy, her speech is halting at best, with phrases and words wrung painfully out of silence.

For someone with a disability, there are daily indignities. One day, in asking my help to decipher something on a menu that confused her, she turned to me suddenly and, with a tear in her eye, said, "Me—you read." She was reminding me that she had taught me to read.

Yet when people meet her, they are surprised at the force of her personality. Through the veil of wordlessness, my mother makes clear her thoughts, her judgments, her ideas. There is frustration enough, God knows, but she did not permit the collapse of her body to collapse her personality. There were times of depression, of unmeasurable sadness. But she rebuilt on her loss. She is not the same person she was before. Some things cannot be reclaimed. Still, there are truths she teaches, things she knows that she did not know before. If we are strong enough, we see that when a dream vanishes it leaves wisdom in its wake.

The day comes, and Jacob must face his brother. They meet. Esau falls upon his neck and weeps.

Why does Esau weep? Years ago my father made a beautiful suggestion. He pointed out that although they did not look alike, Jacob and Esau were twins. Looking into each other's faces, surely they suddenly must have been reminded how old they themselves had grown. They saw etched in each other's eyes the wasted years, the hatred that consumed them. For so much loss, there was nothing to do but weep.

Jacob has lost that most cherished of dreams—that he will be protected and safe. He recognizes that Esau could have killed him. The dream that the world will be kind has fled with each step of his journey. First he discovers that he will achieve only with effort. Then he realizes that the vigor of his youth will disappear. He recognizes that life has slipped out from beneath his grasp. Finally, the promise he extracted from God, that he would be shielded, cannot prove true forever. Is it any wonder that he replies to Pharaoh by commenting on the bitterness of his life? Jacob has suffered genuine losses, it is true. But even more, Jacob is no longer made warm by dreams.

Many of the dreams of youth are dreams that never could have been. The sandlot player had no chance to reach the big leagues; the schoolgirl lacked the gifts to become a great poet. Although that was preordained—talent is a sparse commodity—the day of realization is painful. Dreams are not parceled out only to those with the means to fulfill them. All can dream, though few can fulfill. For every dream that is fulfilled, hundreds are edited, pared down, forgotten, broken, lost.

Dreams can be transformed. Like a sketch taking shape under the artist's hand—which is so different from what we envisioned when we saw the first strong strokes, and yet so right when it finally presents itself—dreams can take shapes we could not have anticipated. An aspiring artist finds his satisfaction in the creation of children in place of canvases; a hopeful starlet is fulfilled by being the center of an enterprise, a business, a charity, which fulfills the same needs as the earlier, misty career.

Dreams, like magical beasts of mythology, change and come

out new. By the time I finished elementary school, I wanted to be a writer. I like to tell stories. I always imagined that I would write novels.

In college, my main interest in religion was to debunk it. Matters of faith did not touch my writing life. But somehow over the years, the dream of writing was redirected into writing about what I had learned from faith and, through others, about life. It was not the writing I imagined when I sat in my college apartment with my covered cardboard and plywood furniture, my charred coffee pot and single burner, banging out stories on an old electric typewriter. The dream was not lost; like water diverted from its stream, it found a new direction to flow.

Sometimes our dreams are not really our own. We think we are living our own dream but it is really one that has come to us from our parents, who see in their children what they could not attain. It is hard for me to look at my daughter and not dream my own dreams through her. As Jung wisely said, the greatest influence on children is the unlived lives of their parents.

Part of my father's drive to success lay in the fact that when his father died, he and his mother found rafts of unpaid bills stuffed in a drawer. My grandfather was no businessman. He started out in vaudeville, a song-and-dance man, a raconteur, a light-hearted man. But after his death, many of his relatives thought him a failure. The implicit burden came down to my father, an only child. He would prove that Ben Wolpe's son was a success.

No child lives entirely his or her own life. How many stage mothers, frustrated in their own dreams to act or sing, push their children forward to live out what they themselves never did? How many immigrants dreamed of their children becoming

professionals—and worked in sweatshops and hovels to ensure
that result? The children lived their parents' dreams, sometimes
happily, sometimes with resentment and regret.

Jacob has not attained all he wished. In the fashion of parents, however, he foists his dreams on those who follow. Tread
softly, wrote Yeats, for you tread on my dreams. Children tread
on the dreams of their parents, sometimes softly, sometimes
with the heedless step of those rushing toward different dreams.
Both children and parents can prove reckless in their hopes.
Jacob has unwittingly bequeathed the ambiguous legacy of
dreams to his favored child. For Joseph, notes struck in his
father's life have eerie echoes in the remarkable tale of the son.

The young dream of what they might be, how they might
transform all they see. They dream of conquests small and large,
of abilities that will expand, magic unsheathed before an unsus-
pecting world. Feeling at times neither honored nor understood,
the young dream of a day when they will command honor and
understanding. They dream, as do we all, of love.

I know someone who as a young girl used to dream that her
parents were not her real parents. She felt far from them, and
imagined that they had found her washed up on the seashore
atop a chest filled with treasure. She imagined great details—
that she must have been from royalty, from a good, kind family.
Someday, she dreamed, they would find her, or she would find
them, and she would live happily ever after.

Dreams of youth are so potent because the line between the
hope inside our own heads and the hardened world outside is
not so clear. When boundaries are blurry, imagination changes

the world. Superheroes of children's comic books are projec-
tions of the child's imagining the power to change the world.
For a moment, the bath towel becomes a cape, and the trash-
can lid a shield that can fend off missiles. External reality slips.
What begins inside a child's head can overflow into the world.
Terrors and wonders are real. A pinecone becomes a magic tal-
isman. And sometimes dreams do make a happy ending. This
young woman dreamed of different parents because her family
was very troubled. Her parents eventually divorced. She forgot
all about her childhood imaginings of happy endings and fairy-
tale dreams.

When I met her years later, she told me that she had indeed
found the kind of family she had dreamed about. She found it
in the family she made for herself, in her husband and child.

The most prominent dream in the Bible that lies on the boundary between childhood and youth is that of Joseph, the son of
Jacob. Joseph dreams of twelve stars in the sky bowing down to
him. Each represents one of his older brothers. Although mil-
lennia separate us from this biblical character, we instinctively
understand his dream. He feels neglected, and he feels special.
As the youngest, he imagines that his brothers will pay homage
to him. Secure in the affections of his father, he turns his brothers' dismissal into a haughty antagonism. He has the arrogance
of the outsider who sneers at what he craves; the one at the party
who refuses to dance because he is afraid he will not have
another chance, because refusal is permanent and therefore safe.
Joseph's brothers may not love him, but he is better, he will rule
over them. And not only his brothers; he dreams of his parents

bowing down. Joseph's dreams are part of a long line of dreams born of resentment mixed with pride. He has the hubris of a dreamer, but he also has the dreamer's sprinkling of particular grace.

Joseph inherits Jacob's talent for dreaming. Like his father, Joseph is a remarkable blend of precocity and self-regard. Joseph's dreams take him to Egypt, where, ultimately, they are fulfilled.

The reason Joseph climbs to the top of the ladder in Egypt is that he proves himself capable of interpreting Pharaoh's dreams. Pharaoh has two dreams: one of skinny cows devouring fat cows, the other of scrawny stalks of grain devouring healthy stalks. No one in the land can adequately interpret the dreams.

Joseph is now in jail, having rejected the sexual advances of his employer's wife. She lied about him and had him imprisoned. While in jail, he has taken to interpreting the dreams of some of his fellow prisoners, including the cupbearer to Pharaoh. When the cupbearer hears of Pharaoh's uninterpreted dreams, he remembers Joseph. Summoned from prison, the young stranger supplies the proper interpretation of Pharaoh's dreams—that there will be seven years of plenty in the land followed by seven years of famine.

The exile thus again becomes involved with dreams, but this time they are someone else's dreams. Joseph rises in the world not when he dreams his own dream, but when he learns to pay attention to the dreams of others. The aspirations of others also can be a key to unlocking our own dreams.

Joseph seems to have lost his own dream. Yet his service to Pharaoh will result in his becoming the vizier of Egypt, and his brothers will indeed come and bow before him, as he had predicted many years before. Seemingly losing his dream has enabled him to focus on the dream of another, returning him, ultimately, to himself.

The flip side of losing our dreams so that they grow is fulfilling our dreams only to discover they are not so satisfying as we imagined. What we lose, then, is the anticipation of perfect happiness that will come if our dreams are realized. Instead we begin to recognize that the charm of a dream is sometimes in the dreaming.

Joseph gets what he wished for. Yet at the end of his life, Joseph, like his father, is not happy. He has lost something through realizing his dream. He has lost the belief that by gaining power he will gain love. He has felt his brothers' hatred, and so dreamed of having power over them, but what he really wants is not their submission but their love. When Joseph's brothers finally bow down to him, Joseph feels none of the glee of triumph we would have seen in his youth. Remarkably, when Joseph sees his brothers after so many years, the first thing he remembers is his dreams—not his brothers' cruelty or betrayal, but his dreams (Gen. 42:9). He knows now that when dreams come true, they prove very different from what one expects.

Though Joseph dies in Egypt, the land of his fame, he has asked to be buried in Israel, just as his father had. Egypt is magnificent, but it cannot be his home. He is separate and alone.

Joseph is special, but his specialness costs him. He suffers for shining. In a transparently autobiographical fragment written in his journal, the poet Delmore Schwartz reflects on Joseph's dilemma.

The gift is loved but not the gifted one;
The coat of many colors is much admired
By everyone, but he who wears the coat
Is not made warm.

Two friends of mine have known each other since childhood. Yet it took many years for them to discover, to their amazement, that they love each other. They both had been too focused on their lives in the world. He was a builder, and she an actress. Her dream was to be a star.

He devoted most of his time and energy to building innovative structures for children with diseases. It consumed him. He was bursting with new ideas about how to help kids who are disabled, how to construct things that would make their lives easier. Much of his time was taken up with charity work, from which he gained nothing but satisfaction.

Their love grew when she caught his dream. It became clear that she would not be able to pursue her career the way she had, with the single-minded determination it required, if they were to marry. But she reinvented herself through his dream. She could help with the children, even perform for them. She was losing her dream, perhaps temporarily, perhaps forever. But in that loss she felt an inestimable gain. Her life, she insisted, had meaning far beyond what it had been before. She lost her dream, but not really; it changed and grew, as it turned from stardom to service.

Joseph's life illustrates how losing our own dreams for the sakes of others can sometimes lead to the realization of what we ourselves desire. But it equally reminds us that what we lose in achieving our dreams sometimes can be profound. In fulfilling our dreams, we also lose them. The dream vanishes once it is complete.

Along the path to fulfilling a dream, we are waylaid by the dreams of others and by our own shortcomings. Emerson wrote in his journal that once in conversation, Thoreau remarked that as long as a man gets in his own way, everything seems to get in his way. Sometimes the world robs us of our dreams. But as often, I suspect, we steal them from ourselves.

Our circle of aspiration narrows as we recognize the dimensions of our original dreams. The story is told of Rabbi Hayim Halberstam, who said that when he was young, he decided to change the world. Discovering that the world was a large place and his efforts were not sufficient, he decided instead to change the people of his town. Even they proved recalcitrant, so in time he resolved to concentrate on changing his family. But by now his children were mostly grown, and his wife knew him far too well to listen to his preaching. "Now," he declared, "I am an old man, and I have realized that I must begin on myself."

The first obstacle to our dreams is ourselves. My father was right about my chess playing. I dreamed of playing far better than I did, but I did not work the way better chess players worked, did not devote the hours of intricate study to the game. Instead, I took the easy route of frustrated dreamers—I envied those who had what I did not. I was jealous of better players, assuming it was all native talent. Some of it was native talent, of course, but even the most gifted player was rigorous, too.

That our dreams might be realized can scare us. Frightened of the possibility that they will come true, we subvert them.

How many talented people undermine their own possibilities with behavior that has no object other than self-sabotage?

This is an underground message of the book of Jonah, about the prophet who seeks to run away from God. God instructs Jonah to prophesy to a city, but Jonah does not wish to play the part of a prophet. Part of what frightens him, I believe, is his own power. With six words he changes the fate of an entire city. The power is too much for him to bear. If he escapes, he will avoid not only facing God but facing Jonah. Better to live small and feel safe. Better not to dream, or to scorn the dreams we have so they do not terrify us.

Underneath every dream is a second dream—the dream of what it will be like if what we wish for is realized. Sometimes people cannot face that scenario, so they flee.

From this fear of realized dreams comes a curiosity in the history of achievement: People do great things and then step back, as if scared by their own deeds. Darwin developed his theory of evolution but did not publish it for more than twenty years. Bobby Fischer won the world championship of chess and then stopped playing. Greta Garbo withdrew from the world of movies at the height of her fame. J. D. Salinger did the same, not only avoiding all public notice but publishing nothing after his early books. Rossini, at the peak of his career as a composer, stopped writing for more than three decades. Why?

While no single reason is adequate for explaining the behaviors of such different people, one thread runs through: The culmination of the dream was not what each expected. Surely none, at the beginning of his or her career, assumed that as triumph bloomed, he or she would withdraw. But the dream is lost in its realization.

We also lose dreams because the dreams themselves are miscast. We do not know ourselves, or the world, deeply enough. When later we lose the dream, the loss is peculiar—it is the loss of what never could have been.

When we lose false dreams, those that never really could have come true—dreams like mine of becoming a baseball player—faith takes on a special role. We wonder if each person exists in order to fulfill a special mission. The human soul is not mass produced. Each of us is unique, and each one's purpose unique. Faith is the assurance that there is a dream and a purpose in life that each person can fulfill. Difficult as it may be to believe at times, the world is large enough to provide a dream that will be meaningful and possible. Our talents may not be what we first thought they were, but they exist—our aims are not incommensurate with our means.

With all the wisdom in the world, however, we will still dream dreams that the world does not help us to realize.

The medieval poet Abraham Ibn Ezra lamented that if he sold candles, the sun would never set, and if he sold burial shrouds, no one would die.

The horrors of the world alone can dissuade people from pursuing dreams, knowing they must be shipwrecked against reality. An idealistic young man I knew in college went to medical school, hoping to set up a chain of clinics in underdeveloped countries. But he took off time to join the Peace Corps and actually saw the lands where he intended to invest his dreams. The magnitude of the squalor and despair paralyzed him. He returned foreswearing the idealism of his youth.

Instead he chose to practice in a small Southern town. To this day he debates whether his abandonment of the dream was the product of the cruelty of the world or the naïveté of the dreamer.

If life steals our faith at the same time it beats down our dreams, then our dreams will disappear. Arthur started several businesses. After a promising beginning, each business failed. They all failed for unrelated reasons that had nothing to do with his competence. When Arthur finally came to see me, he was through dreaming.

"Rabbi, I am going to work for someone else, draw a salary, and forget about creating something of my own," he told me.

The dashed dreams had robbed him of his faith in his mission in the world, and in the world's goodness. He no longer could dream, because his dreams had led to failure.

It was not important that he begin a new business, although in the end he did just that, and so far with success. More important was to restore faith in the possibility of success and joy in the world.

Failure is not the nemesis of dreams, although it seems to be at first glance. Rather, through failure, dreams often grow. The Talmud remarks, "One cannot acquire Torah who has not failed in it." The times when we feel utterly defeated are the moments when we have the chance to see farther, to reach down deeper into ourselves, to acquire wisdom. It is the time to begin dreaming wise dreams.

There is no end to the chronicle of those who found failure a stepping-stone to greater accomplishment. In every case, people needed faith, ultimately, to sustain themselves. Winston Churchill, who was by some measure the most successful man of our century, knew failure all too well. His trials began early, when at age eighteen he fell almost thirty feet, rupturing a kidney and remaining unconscious for three days. At age forty, he was deposed as first Lord of the Admiralty; most assumed his career was over, and he himself confided to a friend, "I'm finished." Seven years later, Churchill had fought his way back to Parliament and a position in the Cabinet. While he was in the hospital for an operation, he was voted out of office. As he later said, "In the twinkling of an eye, I found myself without an office, without a seat, without a party, and without an appendix." A friend who dined with him that week found him so depressed he could hardly speak.

Ten years later, Churchill was sick, having lost a fortune and without any position in his party. He told his wife he thought he would never recover from the triple blow. Yet seven years after those reversals, he was back in the Admiralty he had left nearly a quarter century before, and on the verge of his blaze of glory.

Was Churchill a failure? Absolutely. And also a glorious triumph. Beneath his depression, he had an abiding faith in his mission in this world. In typically wry fashion, he once said, "We are all worms, but I do believe I am a glowworm." Churchill knew he had a place and purpose in this world. He had faith.

Failure is a loss of dreams, the loss of what we thought might be. It can be devastating. Say the word out loud—"fail"—and hear its power. It suggests a certain totality, as if to fail is to be little or nothing. But as Rabbi Johanan teaches in the Midrash we quoted at the beginning of this chapter, the eye has a light part and a dark part; one can see only through the dark part. We see through darkness, through failure, if outside there is light. In other words, if we move through failure with faith, it can become a powerful shaper of character. Yousef Karsch, the portraitist who photographed many celebrated men and women of this century (including a well-known portrait of Churchill), concluded from his encounters with so many famous people that "character, like a photograph, develops in darkness."

Learning from failure should be central to our lives, but we are so frightened of failure we ignore it and forget it. Corporations from all over the world are suddenly calling on the Army's Center for Army Lessons Learned, created in the aftermath of the conflict in Grenada. Realizing that failure is a rich mine for learning, the Army established a center to discover how failure can be turned to benefit.

The Maggid (storyteller) of Dubnov used to tell of a king who had a precious diamond. He would take out the diamond each night to marvel at its beauty and perfection. One night, to his horror, he dropped it and saw a small crack had developed from its base to its crown.

Panicked, he summoned all the craftsmen of the kingdom to plead with them to repair his diamond. They all insisted it could not be done—a diamond, once cracked, is irreparable. The king initiated a search throughout the kingdom for anyone who could fix his jewel. Eventually a humble jeweler in the outer provinces of the kingdom saw the notice and volunteered to help the king. The king showed him the diamond and asked if he could fix it when everyone else had failed. The jeweler assured him that he could. "If you fix this," the king said, his voice shaking, "I will give you unimaginable riches. But if you fail, you will be killed for deceiving the king."

The man went into isolation under the king's guard and began to work. Days passed, then weeks, then months. Finally he emerged. There was great fanfare in the city as the time came to unveil the diamond. With trembling hands, the king took the wrapping off his jewel. He saw that the crack was still there, just as before. In fury he called for the jeweler's head. But the jeweler calmly told the king to turn his diamond over.

Turning it over, the king saw what he had not noticed before. At the very top of the diamond, the man had carved petals, so that now the crack was not a flaw but the stem of a flower, making the diamond even more beautiful.

Not all flaws can be made into flowers, but each failure can be a chance to make something more beautiful, more profound, than it was before. When we lose the dream of what should have been, we are given the gift of what might be.

In the Bible, old age might almost be called the time of blessings that will not be realized. For final dreams can be visions of perfection, wishing the world to be more than it is, or perhaps ever can be. The fervid dreams of the dying prove beyond the efforts of those left behind.

At the very end of his life, Moses offers a final farewell to the people Israel. He exhorts them to be good, to follow God's way, to prosper in the promised land that he will not live to see. Moses summons all the reserves of his eloquence, learned through a lifetime of fidelity to God's word. He seeks to conjure up a faithful and glorious future.

The irony lurking behind Moses' words is that the children of Israel will surely disobey God, **and Moses knows it.** Even as Moses pleads with the people, God's words from a previous chapter must recur in his head: "The Lord said to Moses: 'You are soon to lie with your ancestors. The people will then go astray after alien gods in their midst, in the land they are about to enter. They will forsake Me and break My covenant that I made with them' " (Deut. 31:16). Moses knows enough about the Israelites, and about human nature, to recognize that wisdom is a fragile inheritance. For every time wise words are heeded, there are scores of times when they are disregarded or misapplied. At the beginning of his great speech, Ha'azinu, Moses calls heaven and earth to witness his words (Deut. 32:1). Perhaps those witnesses are necessary because he knows that human beings will forget. Moses faces failure at the last moments of his life, and converts that failure into an enduring poem of witness.

Moses' dream is the dream of all those who care for what they leave behind. It is an ethical will, written for those who will come later, to remind them of what is important.

In our last stage of life, we dream of legacy versus oblivion. For all the dreams that have been lost in life, there are some we wish to see endure. Listen, for example, to the words of the great and vigorous King Alfred, advising the inhabitants of his kingdom to create their own ease, in the ninth century C.E.

> *Then I gathered for myself staves and props and bars, and handles for all the tools I knew how to use, and crossbars and beams for all the structures I knew how to build, and the fairest piece of timber I knew how to carry. I neither came home with a single load, nor did it suit me to bring home all the wood, even if I could have carried it. In each tree I saw something that I required at home. For I advise each of us who are strong and have many wagons, to plan to go to the same wood where I have cut these props, and fetch for himself more there,*

and load his wagons with fair rods, so that he can plait many a fair wall, and put up many a peerless building, and build a fair enclosure with them, and may dwell therein pleasantly and at his ease, winter and summer, as I have not yet done.

The pathos of that last phrase, "as I have not yet done," strikes us across the centuries. Alfred pictures a time when he will live in quiet in his own sturdily constructed home—a modest dream, though we may doubt if it was granted to this king, who died in his mid-fifties during a turbulent time. Having done so much for his people, he envisions a time when they, as he, will be able to reap the fruits of his lifetime of effort.

For Moses, the dream is lost as he pronounces it. A subtle despair darkens his words. Alone and at the point of death, Moses must plead with his people, knowing they will not listen after he is gone.

Moses builds on this recognition. He does not succumb to it. There is anger in his words, and disappointment, but no despair. He speaks to those who will betray his dream. Yet he knows that the betrayal of the dream is not forever, that the vision will outlast its traducers. Moses overcomes his loss with love. He cares passionately about the people to whom he has given so much. Even in his final farewell, knowing what will befall them, he holds them close.

There is no isolation in the world, no dream that affects only the dreamer. As we have seen, the dreams of Jacob and Joseph profoundly affected their families and, ultimately, the world. At times we imagine that our dreams are single strings on the

instrument of ourselves, that we are playing solo. In the har-
monies of the world, however, every dream is a concert.

Our dreams interpenetrate. Sometimes we even find that the
dream we thought we had lost is alive in someone else, who can
return it to us. That is illustrated by the following charming tale.

Reb Eisek, son of Reb Yekel, dreamed that a treasure was
buried beneath a certain bridge in Prague. Spurred by his
poverty, he traveled all the way to Prague, but when he came
upon the bridge, he found that it was guarded by soldiers.
Unable to dig, and left with no other choice, he told the captain his dream. The captain laughed, and said, "Why, if we followed every dream, I'd follow mine—that there was a treasure
buried under the stove in the house of a Jew named Eisek son of
Yekel from Cracow!" Reb Eisek went home and dug up a treasure from under his stove.

We do not dream only for one another, however. We dream
as a collective, and the collective dreams are some of the hard-
est and most powerful to realize. Among the greatest dreams of
humanity is the drive to know, to unravel the mysteries of this
world. Alongside that hope is the dream for an end to the savagery, hatred, and strife that have plagued us since our first steps
on earth.

The greatest dream is also the greatest disappointment: the
dream of salvation in this world, of a human order both joyous
and just, of a world ungnarled by viciousness and anguish. The
Messiah is not only a national dream, although it often has been
expressed as the aspirations of a nation. The Messiah is also a

global dream and a personal dream. The Messiah represents a liberation from the darkness of history.

The hope for redemption is the most basic dream. Its kernel is the promise that the travail of this world will be overcome, that the darkness will give way to dawn, that humanity will stride toward a different future. For most of history, the world has been an unspeakable place, and it still is for so many human beings. Ancient and medieval writings speak to us of a time of daily fears. Listen to a great medieval historian, Marc Bloch, writing of the epoch of knights and castles.

> [In the Middle Ages] the wild animals that now only haunt our nursery tales—bears, and above all wolves—prowled in every wilderness, and even amongst the cultivated fields. So much was this the case that the sport of hunting was indispensable for ordinary security, and almost equally so as a method of supplementing the food supply. People continued to pick wild fruit and gather honey as in the first ages of mankind . . . The nights, owing to the wretched lighting, were darker; the cold, even in the living quarters of the castles, was more intense. In short, behind all social life there was a background of the primitive, of submission to uncontrollable forces . . . Infant mortality was undoubtedly very high . . . As to the life of adults, even apart from the hazards of war it was usually short by our standards . . . Old age seemed to begin very early, as early as mature adult life with us. The world which considered itself very old, was in fact governed by young men.

Bloch goes on to speak of epidemics, famine, and rampant violence. Is it any wonder that our predecessors had a very different view of life? The ancient world bore the same trials. Ecclesiastes, in a moment when his cynicism slips into despair, says that it is best not to be born.

In such a world, the promise of the Messiah represented an ease in the moral struggle and an abatement of suffering. An age of peace.

Messianism is a dream of faith, but not of faith alone. Even those who find themselves without faith hope for an age when somehow the perfections we envisage will spread over the landscape of our suffering, and the world will be better. Many who have lost faith in God retain faith in a messianic age. It is one of the most durable dreams of the human heart.

We wait for the Messiah, and the Messiah does not come. There are even jokes about the man who stands on the watchtower of the town—his job is to wait for the Messiah. Someone asks him, "Do you do it for the pay?" "No," he answers, "the pay is lousy." "Well, then, you must get a lot of respect for this position." "No," answers the man, "people give me no respect at all." "Then why do you do it?" he is asked. "Well, it is steady work."

There is a strange statement in the Midrash that the Messiah will not come until the tears of Esau are exhausted. Dreamers like Jacob can be too zealous in realizing their dreams. The effects of those dreams can persist in ways the dreamer never imagined. Jacob's dream involved Esau's pain. Not until we lose certain dreams will others be made real.

The Messiah is a dream that everyone can understand instinctively. All of us at certain times are tempted to despair. "Do not despair" was the motto of one of the most profound and remarkable Hasidic rabbis, Nachman of Bratzlav.

As Rabbi Nachman lay dying, his disciple tells us, these were his words: "'Do not despair! There is no such thing as despair at all!' He drew forth these words slowly and deliberately and with such strength and wondrous depth that he taught everyone, for all generations, that no one should despair, no matter what he has to endure."

Rabbi Nachman's teaching is the very foundation of faith, that for all the trials of the world, life can be made worthwhile if only we do not abandon the belief that life can be made worthwhile. We are the prophets of our own destinies; that which we believe will be meaningful will be meaningful. When we despair, we empty the world of meaning for our lives.

Rabbi Nachman's biographer, Arthur Green, closes his book by quoting the historian Emmanuel Ringelblum's diary of the Warsaw ghetto: "In the prayer house of the Hasidim from Bratzlav on Nowolipie Street there is a large sign: 'Jews, Never Despair!' The Hasidim dance there with the same religious fervor as they did before the war."

Life bids each of us to acknowledge and let go of the dreams that cannot be. It is easy to become so fond of the impossible dream that we live our lives bemoaning what is not instead of creating what might be. We release old dreams like old friends, realizing at times that we have grown apart, saying good-bye with regret but also with the knowledge that life must be lived, not simply recalled.

Dreams, personal and global, thread through our lives. When we take them as challenges, they can re-enchant our lives. The best dreams outlive our own lives. There is a story about an old man planting a tree in his garden. Someone walks by and calls out, "Old man, why are you planting that tree? You will never live to see it bear fruit." "True," answers the man, "but my ancestors planted for me, and I am planting for those who will come after me."

Dreams can ennoble us even when they fail, even when they are lost, even when we let them go. Each dream can be a step on the ladder we climb in order to become the person we were meant to be.

Four

———————

Self

If I am I because you are you, then I am not I and you are not you.
But if I am I because I am I, and you are you because
you are you, then I am I and you are you.
—Rabbi Menachem Mendel of Kotzk

I once had a student who lost herself. She had grown up in Europe and then moved to Los Angeles. She was a sweet, smart woman who was not sure what she wanted. In time, the seductions of the culture here began to work on her. Abandoning her plans for a teaching career, she decided to change who she was. She began to wear makeup and long nails and traded in her simple clothes for elaborate outfits. She met and married someone very wealthy. Her life began to revolve around restaurants and cosmetic counters.

Perhaps her transformation would have been fine had it reflected her true nature. But it was a function of the people with whom she surrounded herself. She no longer could find the boundary between who she was and who others wished her to be.

Before she got married, I asked if she would come to my office. There we had a long talk. I told her that I thought a part of her self was disappearing, a beautiful and valuable part, and I hoped she would cherish it and not forget it. In later years she was still split, a piece of her dissatisfied, still wanting to be a teacher, and a piece of her unable to renege on the many pleasures her chosen life offered.

This young woman lost herself, but not productively. She did not find someone who could reflect back to her what was noble and best in her. Part of our task in life is to choose worthy companions who will cultivate what is good in us. We choose clothes to highlight our best features, we turn our best side to the camera, but it is easy to forget that the people we surround ourselves with are not only those whom we find interesting— they are the ones to whom we give the privilege of helping shape who we are.

Everyone with whom we come into prolonged contact will make demands upon us. What is asked of us is critical to the choices we make. How comfortable we feel in responding honestly to those demands will determine the integrity of our lives.

When we respond to another's demands *because* they are another's demands, and not because we recognize their truth or justice, a small piece of who we are is stretched, twisted, becomes unrecognizable. People with strong selves react instinctively, knowing whether something is good and whether it suits their needs. If they choose to go against what they feel, they do so deliberately and consciously, not out of fear or a desire to please. My student was not just under the influence of people whose values were different from her own; she was sabotaged by her inability to hold tight to who she was.

The sociologist David Riesman wrote about inner- and outer-directed people. Inner-directed people are those who, usually through childhood training, have a core set of values. No matter the situations in which those people are placed, their values determine their choices. Outer-directed people respond to the situation. They are more flexible. They do not butt heads as often with the world. But they are not the people who live the deepest lives or who teach the world to be better or to change. They have adaptability, but not true strength. They cannot live as deeply, because their selves are always being clouded by others' needs or wishes. They know how to prosper, but not how to lead.

America contributes to outer direction. The breakdown of traditional communities means that fewer people will have a powerful inheritance of values. The day when children grew up with the church or synagogue being the primary conduit of values, or when the public school espoused a set of clear values, is gone. Moreover, outside influences are so strong, and material successes so great, that people will more naturally be flexible.

Outer-directed people have a weakened sense of self. All of us are pulled outside our selves at times. We see something that does not really conform to our values, but we are enchanted by it. But if the self is strong enough, it is not like iron but like elastic, and it will regain its shape. If it is too inflexible, it will snap; if too unformed, it will dissolve.

Being pulled temporarily out of shape is not the same as being lost. Losing the self is a creative, fruitful dissolution of boundaries. When we lose ourselves, we come to realize the enormity and wonder of what exists. This experience has been described as an oceanic feeling; we are drops in the boundless sea. Like all tremendous experiences, it can be bewildering. Sometimes it leads to stupidities and excesses. Growing is not always controllable and tidy. But this sort of loss is possible only for one who begins with a strong sense of self.

When I counsel people, I keep in mind the technique of *bittul hayesh*, the nullification of the self. I try to enter the other person, to understand from his or her life and ideals what the challenge means. I cannot guide someone from inside myself alone. I need rather to take what I know and seek—as far as possible—to nullify myself and to embrace the other's outlook and life situation. In order to do so, however, I have to be sure that I am firm enough to speak truthfully, and to know who I am.

All of us feel instinctively that there is a self inside, yet we know that the self changes throughout life. Are we a fixed nature, or shifting? My reading of the world, and the traditions I have learned, teaches me that we are given a certain nature, that each self is unique. Yet each self also is capable of being shaped. We take the rudiments that are ours alone, and we mold them by contact with others, by conduct of life, by intention, and by circumstance. At some point in our lives, we learn that to really discover who we are, we have to go through the process of losing ourselves to find ourselves; in the moment when everything drops out and disappears, suddenly from within we begin to forge a new and greater understanding of who we are. It is when we seek above ourselves, beyond ourselves, that we most truly find ourselves.

In the Bible, the story of Saul is the chronicle of a loss of self. Perhaps more accurately, it is the story of a man who, in a strange way, *cannot* lose himself. Saul is a tall, handsome, strapping figure of a man. He is chosen by God to be the new king.

Yet early on there are hints that Saul does not possess a solid sense of self. At the moment he is about to be crowned king of Israel, he is cowering behind barrels.

What happens when someone who is uncertain inside, whose soul trembles, is put in a position of power? Gradually the position itself becomes the prop that holds him up. So it becomes with Saul. Lacking a rich, resonant sense of his own character, he becomes the king. When that position is threatened, so is the foundation of his personhood. His self crumbles.

The threat comes in the form of David: young, ambitious, talented, vital. David comes to the court as a support for Saul's soul. David plays his harp and soothes the king's melancholy.

But not for long. Soon Saul realizes that the qualities he has found in David have been seen by others as well. Prodigies become threats when others recognize their magic. So long as Saul alone loves David, all is peaceful. In time, however, David becomes loved by the people. As David's fame and power advance, Saul is threatened.

Madness grips Saul, and he seeks to end David's life. Saul becomes unable to see beyond himself. For sometimes the madness that accompanies the collapse of selfhood is not the inability to see oneself, but the inability to see anything but oneself, to believe in the reality of others. The person who suffers from extreme paranoia does not acknowledge the reality of others. Others become little more than cartoon characters in a private fantasy. In Ibsen's *Peer Gynt*, the superintendent of the insane asylum says of the inmates:

> *Outside? No, there you are strangely mistaken!*
> *It's here, sir, that one is oneself with a vengeance; oneself, and nothing whatever*

besides. We go, full sail, as our very selves. Each one shuts himself up in the barrel of self, in the self-fermentation he dives to the bottom, with the self-bung he seals it hermetically, and seasons the staves in the well of self. No one has tears for the other's woes; no one has mind for the other's ideas.

Counseling families in times of grief, I have often seen this drama unfold. When people are grieving, other people become almost unreal. The pain is so overwhelming that to recognize the reality of others is too great an emotional burden. Sometimes the eyes of someone in deep pain will look at you with the unfocused stare that lets you know you are not being seen. I ask the mourner questions and get no answers, or distracted answers. Later on the mourner will say that the time of death and shortly after was almost like a dream. The world was lifted from its usual moorings, and everything became unreal—especially other people.

After officiating at a funeral, I stood beside a man who had lost his father. His father was not old, in his early sixties, and the man had been quite affected by the loss. We had spent several hours talking about his father the previous few days, and now as we stood together beside the grave and I was about to leave, he turned to me and said, quite seriously, "Rabbi, I certainly hope to meet you one day." Perhaps it was a slip of the tongue. Maybe he meant to say "meet you again." But in the slip was truth. We had met on a profound level, and in another way not at all. He was curled up in loss; for him, the time we had spent together was about his relationship to his father and little else.

Saul is stopped up in a cask of self. Rarely he emerges. When David demonstrates that he could have killed Saul but did not

(I Sam. 24), Saul temporarily regains his sanity, which is to say, his self. But the recovery is brief.

Finally the denouement is played out. In a scene of subtle terror, Saul—who has explicitly forbidden recourse to divination, to mediums and witches—goes to a fortune-teller. There he summons up the prophet Samuel from the depths, and discovers that he is to die in battle the next day.

Saul's death is the culmination of a special kind of tragedy. His opportunities outstrip his cohesiveness as a character. It is as if the pieces of his being cannot be kept together. Saul loses himself because he cannot manage something so grand and demanding as kingship. Sometimes roles elevate us. We can rise to the level of other people's perception—when we are seen as kings, we walk as kings. But other times, as for Saul, what people ask of us may crush us. We cannot find ourselves anymore under the press of expectation.

The High Priest who first anointed Saul as king was Samuel. Before Samuel's death, he diagnosed Saul's problem in one line: "Are you small in your own eyes? You are the king of Israel, And God has sent you on a journey" (I Sam. 15:17–18).

Saul's sin, his flaw, is that he does not have faith in his own importance. Stricken by the fear that he does not matter, Saul goes mad when he sees someone who is strong and confident. The larger the clothes he puts on, the more he feels his own insufficiency. Saul is like the parent who runs away when the child is born because the reality of the role is too overwhelming. The more real the kingship becomes, the more Saul wants it to disappear. But since he cannot simply divest himself of being king, he spirals deeper and deeper into darkness. When he finally reaches the point where he can no longer deal with the disparity between what he feels and what the world expects of him, he disintegrates. He has lost his self. From such a devastating loss, there is, for Saul, no recovery.

To truly have a self means to give others their selves as well. To have a self means to appreciate that not everything others do is about you or is done with you in mind. To have a self is to remember two seemingly contradictory things at once: that we all are connected and that actions of others may have nothing to do with you. We all may be buds on the universal branch, but others do not flower to spite you.

The anthropologist Claude Lévi-Strauss once remarked that astronomy developed as the first science among human beings because the stars are far away. Anthropology came much later. To study what is distant is easy; to see up close takes time. That is one reason why we are so quick to judge others but often remain mysteries to ourselves. Our gears mesh out of our own sight. We take up the microscope, the binocular, the periscope to see what is outside. What instrument do we use to find what is inside?

One instrument is solitude, the other society. When we are alone, we hear our own voices speak. In the devotional practice of *hitbodedut*, aloneness, the individual finds a place where no one will hear, and talks to God. It may be difficult, but that too is a discovery. In whatever language the person speaks, he or she should address Ultimacy, what is highest in the universe. Of course, one is not "alone," strictly speaking, if God is there. But part of the point is to move from aloneness to a sense of Divine presence.

An ancient Rabbinic book begins with the words "Moses received the Torah from Sinai." Why does it not simply say "Moses received the Torah from God"?

The usual interpretation is that "Sinai" is a kind of spiritual synecdoche: It really means "from God," and the mountain is a metaphor.

But the great medieval commentator Abravanel proposed another answer. Had Moses not spent forty days and nights alone on Sinai, he would not have been able to receive the Torah. The time alone, in prayer and meditation, prepared him for the experience of encountering God. In that moment of greatest intimacy, Moses must be separate from humanity.

Ideally, *hitbodedut* is supposed to be practiced in the forest. Modern life being what it is, I have tried it, of all places, in my car. Sometimes driving alone, I feel free to speak, knowing other people will not hear me. Can God not listen as well on freeways as in forests? Sometimes I am surprised at what wells up inside me. I ask for things I did not know I wanted. I pray in words I am surprised are mine. I feel embarrassed, and then ask myself, before whom am I embarrassed? Myself? Surely not before God, to whom I am saying nothing unknown.

This type of meditative solitude forces us to see inside ourselves. We become the ear that listens to our own words. There is no other person to absorb what we say. It lingers. We come to know ourselves also through serious encounter with other human beings. Every dialogue can be read as a road map of the self. People help us uncover different facets of ourselves. "I like myself when I am with her" is a phrase I hear over and over again when I meet with couples who are about to marry. The groom has discovered that with this woman, he is someone new—the same, but different. There is a vitality, an eagerness, an ability and desire to love and be loved. But it is not his alone. It lives in the energy that swirls between them.

The couple will discover that to be new people means also that parts of who they were must recede. New facets of the self, in their brilliance, will force others to fade.

Great tales of self-discovery are tales of unfolding. Yet they are tales also of discarding. As we grow, pieces of our selves seem to fall off and float away, like autumn leaves on a lake.

Just as we must lose ourselves to find out who we are, parts of ourselves must fade in order to make way for new ways of being. The imaginary creatures who populate our childhood world cannot live on in the same way in our adult world.

From the time we are small, we assume certain roles. The role of being a child is a comfortable one, and often we are loath to leave it behind. A young man who came to my office complained that his father controlled his life. Yet each time I tried to get him to do something to pry that control loose, to get a job, to move out, to defy his father's wishes in whatever particular, he balked. Finally I told him that while he chafed under the control, it also made him safe, and he was not willing to give it up. I told him that leaving is indispensable to growth, and recounted the story of two rabbis, each of whom had the same teacher. One of them slavishly, exactly, duplicated the teacher's words and decisions throughout his life. The second developed his own interpretations and ideas. When they met, the first disciple told the second how disappointed he was. "Why could you not follow the way of our master?" he asked. The second said, "Actually, I did follow the way of our master—more faithfully than you. You see, he grew up and left his teacher, and I grew up and left mine."

"Child" is only one of innumerable roles we assume in our lifetimes. We assume roles in response to the uncertainty of being. Upon meeting another, we do not ask "Who are you?" but "What do you do?" The first question is too comprehensive and too weighted. Defining people by roles is safer. Roles are the shorthand of self-presentation. We do not have time to tell one another everything, so we present our social positions and life concerns in a nutshell.

But asking that question is not only a step to knowledge, it is an invitation to refuge. By hiding behind jobs, roles, prescribed activities, we make it impossible for others to look inside our souls. "Who are you?" is a question that we all should wish to ask one another, but in the world as it is, we are rarely interested. And how would we answer such a question when we are unsure ourselves?

I am a rabbi. That is more than an occupation. When people in my community see me on the street, they do not think, *There is David, who spends part of his time being a rabbi.* Instead, unless they know me well or in another context, they think, *There is the rabbi.*

There are wonderful parts to this statement, and parts that are confining. When I was a child, I was not just a child—I was "the rabbi's kid." Adults often would say things to me that were more properly addressed to my father. They would mention, with an embarrassed look, that they really did not keep the Sabbath. I wanted to say, "Look, I am five years old—I don't care!" But early on I understood that in many people's minds, my father's role spilled over onto his children.

Now I have assumed the role for myself, not always comfortably. When I wear casual clothes, people say, "How could the rabbi be wearing jeans?" as though somehow I should always sport a holy wardrobe, or at least dress formally. The rabbi's clothes should match not just the dignity of the role but other people's understandings of that dignity. The role of a rabbi is not shucked off once I leave the office. It is with me wherever I go.

So what part of me is the rabbi, and what part David? There is a confusion, or perhaps a melding of selves. I know that I have lost part of what I was in order to become a rabbi. My father once told me a wonderful story. He was playing golf with some congregants from his synagogue, and one of them started to tell what was obviously an off-color joke. The man stopped himself and said, with surprise, "You know, Rabbi, if you weren't here, could I tell you a joke!" He could tell it to my father as a friend. He could not to my father as a rabbi.

When I was teaching rabbinical students, I saw how many of them were captured by their role. As the training progressed, there was a certain self-regard that crept in to the bearing of many students. They were no longer treated as before— they were invited to speak to people many times their age, and looked up to with expectation. To be simply young students did not seem enough. As people continued to treat them with reverence, the weight rested more fully on their shoulders. Sometimes I could almost hear their voices drop a few decibels.

Our roles can trap us. Indeed, even the best roles can prove harmful precisely because what we are becomes more dependent on the role than on the person. Emerson wrote that he sometimes thought the best part of a man revolts against being a preacher: "His good revolts against official goodness."

As we work through the roles of our lives, we ask ourselves what is essential to the self. Which losses should we happily sustain, and which should we mourn? Which should we accede to, and which should we refuse on all grounds?

There is a spiritual self, a self of highest values and aspirations, which we should not forfeit to any role or request or demand. That is the part of the self that is connected to something greater than ourselves. It is an instrument for larger forces in the universe to speak to us and through us. That self is the self of faith.

This self is more individual for being less insistent on individuality. All prophets proclaim themselves to be speaking the word of God, but their prophecies differ. One person is a violin, another a flute. The music of the world does not sound the same as it flows through us, for each of us is a unique instrument. In order to find our tone, we have to shed selves and try on new ones, to be alone and interact with others. All the while, however, we must aim toward the refinement of our own music, the growth of our own soul.

At the age of forty-five, Sherwood Anderson found himself the manager of a small paint factory in Elyria, Ohio. One day, in the middle of a sentence he was dictating, he walked out of the factory and gave himself to literature. Writing his books, which he believed expressed the best part of himself, was a process of discovery by loss.

There is no waste in God's world. There is no soul without a
mission. There have been times when I feel the universe at my
back, in a sense, which suggests I am doing something that is in
harmony with something greater than myself. When I feel discouraged, I can sometimes revive myself with the thought that
if there were not a unique role for each person, it would be
senseless for all of us to be different.

Searching for that purpose is a critical lesson in the art of life.

The great scholar Hayyim of Volozhin was not a distin-
guished student at school. One day he told his parents he had
resolved to give up studying and go to trade school. They
agreed, and that night Hayyim had a dream. In his dream, an
angel showed him a pile of books. "Whose books are those?" he
asked. "Yours," replied the angel, "if you will have the courage
to write them."

A friend of mine was faced with this dilemma as a child. His
father was an eminent scientist and decided his son would go
into science. The son balked, and it became a constant source
of friction between them. Finally the father told his son that he
would cut him off if he did not pursue a scientific career. The
son told him that he would then be cut off. As a result, the son
went into business. He built the largest business of his kind in
the country and became, despite his youth, a major donor to
several charitable causes. The same courage that he learned in
shaking off his father's demands served him well in business.
There is no safety like the safety of knowing that one has the
resources inside to endure. That confidence enables us to search
for what is true, rather than what is only safe.

Mary Moody Emerson, Ralph Waldo Emerson's aunt, perhaps
the most important intellectual influence in his life, told him,

"Always do that which you are afraid to do." What are you afraid to do? Which part of life threatens the security of your cloak? What piece of yourself must you lose in order to find yourself?

According to legend, an evil spirit once took the throne away from King Solomon. The king traveled around his kingdom disguised as a beggar. Dressed in rags, he was treated shabbily by people who, the day before, were fawning at his feet. People thought him a lunatic because he claimed he was the king.

He wandered for three years. He ate whatever he could find. He pleaded with people to believe that he really was a king. From city to city, Solomon traveled, reflecting on his life.

The story tells us, however, that Solomon's most difficult moment was when someone *did* recognize him. One man fed Solomon a meal befitting a king and reminisced about the greatness of Solomon's court. The contrast between what he was and what he had become was too much to bear for the dispossessed king, who wept bitterly. Being known in a fallen state was even worse than being unknown. The role was so important to Solomon that he could not feel worthy without it. He had been born in the palace and had never learned what it meant to move through the world without the royal robe.

Solomon regained his throne. But he could not be the same. His equilibrium was forever altered. The world was no longer safe. The king grew to understand what his life would have been had he not been born in the palace. For the first time, Solomon came to face himself.

In this legend, Solomon faces a reality we all fear. What if all the things that make us safe were suddenly gone? What would we find under the roles, the robe, the carefully constructed images of our lives?

The painful, swift change of losing roles can be a means of discovering who we are. At two of the most dramatic moments in the Bible, unrelated moments, the same imagery is used. Immediately after consuming the forbidden fruit, God seeks Adam and Eve in the garden and asks, "Why were you hiding?" Adam answers, "I was afraid because I was naked, so I hid."

The second time the image of nakedness is used is in the book of Job. Job has been battered by the hand of God. He has lost his children, his possessions. Bereft, betrayed by his protector, Job gives his initial reaction. He utters those remarkable words: "Naked came I into this world, and naked shall I return."

Why at these crucial moments is nakedness invoked? Why do Adam and Job, searching for words to describe the extremity, the uttermost reaches of experience, one of pain and one of shame, reach for this same word, *arum*, naked?

Although both Adam and Job refer to nakedness in a literal sense—Job was naked upon birth, and Adam was naked in the garden—most readers of these stories see also a powerful symbolic message. The Rabbis interpret Adam and Eve's nakedness in a curious way: naked of *mitzvot*, naked of good deeds—they have no worthy actions to protect themselves. That interpretation hints at the deeper issue.

Neither story is about physical nakedness. They both are about the interplay between security and vulnerability, nakedness and hiding. Adam is about to be revealed. He has rebelled against God. What do human beings do when they are about to be caught? They hide. They cover themselves. They seek shelter.

When we are ashamed, what do we say? "I want to crawl

into a hole." That means that we do not want to stand naked, revealed.

The metaphors for being revealed are frightening: They found me out. I was exposed. Stripped. I had nowhere to hide. Both Adam and Job remind us how terrifying it is to feel that we cannot conceal ourselves.

Like Adam, like Job, we are always seeking cover. Only in extremes are we forced to feel naked. Feeling naked can be humiliating. Captors strip prisoners not only to search them but to disempower them. Without coverings, we have no way to exaggerate our merits or screen our deficiencies. We feel helpless.

Why do superheroes always have disguises? In comic books and movies, the superhero is never really known. To be perfectly covered, to be disguised, is to be invulnerable. We are left wondering about the identity of Batman, or Zorro, or the Lone Ranger. The cloak of anonymity means that no one can touch the essential you, because you remain withheld. As soon as someone knows the true identity, Bruce Wayne or Clark Kent, the hero is stripped. Omnipotence is lost with identification. To be known is to be human, and therefore frail. Think of the pathetic, cowering Wizard of Oz when the curtain is drawn back. In mystery, he was terrifying. Exposed, he is a figure of fun.

The clothing on our bodies is the symbolic first layer of our hiddenness. When we cloak the physical body, we hide something deeper. We help ourselves to feel secure, protected, not exposed. Grooming oneself is another way of concealing oneself. Do I look okay? Are all the imperfections hidden?

At times we reveal bits of ourselves, but only by calculation. You may have a slit skirt or an unbuttoned shirt—that is not the same as this primal nakedness. It is strategic uncovering—planned for maximum positive affect. Nakedness is beyond affect. There are no more strategies.

Nakedness reveals the part of us we don't want revealed, that we fight against. "Adam," God asks, "where are you?" Adam does not want God to know.

Naked came Job out of his mother's womb. Naked—without defenses. Naked—without mistrust. Naked—without the powerful, almost impenetrable shield that we build around our souls in order to survive in this world.

And I will return naked, says Job. In the end, it all will be taken from me. All my defenses and my ingenuity will not prevent my being taken. I will die, and be naked once more.

It takes catastrophe for Job to feel his nakedness. Having lost his wealth, his physical coverings, Job tries other methods of covering his nakedness, of protecting himself. He wears his anger and indignation like a fur coat. It keeps him warm.

We cover ourselves in a variety of ways. Words help keep us hidden. How many times have we made casual conversation when we are really trembling? Words can push the world away. They'll protect us. Small talk will deflect the glance that sees inside.

When people ask how I am, I say, "I am fine." If I don't feel fine, and they push, I say, "No, really, I am fine." Even if they see that my face belies my words, it is hard for them to keep pressing when I have *told* them I am fine. The words keep them out.

We can use anger as a shield. It will stop any exploration. Try to see inside my center, and I will turn to rage. My insides scream, "Get out!" I will not be revealed.

We use passivity, too. "Whatever you want," we say. Just don't press it. Why are we still talking—I agreed, didn't I? Leave me alone. Don't force me to confront what I want. Don't strip my pretenses.

We use a variety of shields and masks to keep ourselves from being exposed. For we imagine that we might not be, in our core selves, worthy. Better to surround ourselves with the accoutrements of success than to be seen as we truly are. We do not always wish to be naked, even to ourselves. "Know myself?" asked Goethe. "If I knew myself, I'd run away."

It is a remarkable feature of the story of Adam and Eve that their saga as human beings begins with nakedness. Adam is punished, he is expelled from the garden of Eden. But it is only then, after he is punished, that he and Eve have children. The Jewish calendar dates the beginning of recorded time from that moment. Equally, it is after Job recalls his nakedness that he begins the agonizing exploration of faith that is the essence of his story. In a series of dialogues exploring the meaning of evil in the world, Job finds himself in confrontation with his friends, with himself, and with God.

When we are naked and have forfeited our defenses, we begin to see ourselves. The moment need not be as dramatic as the troubles of Job or the sin of Adam. Flashes of understanding come in that painful instant when someone else refuses or rejects; it can happen when we discover we are not equal to the task we have undertaken; it can happen in the instant we realize we have disappointed someone we love. Insight can slip upon us quickly, barely noticed. Such flashes are openings for self-understanding.

Sometimes we lose ourselves to another, and discover that we have in the other found who we are.

Rabbi Nachman of Bratzlav, the great Hasidic weaver of tales, told the following story. Once there was a king who knew a wise man whom he valued and trusted. One day the wise man told the king terrible news: The supply of grain that year was adequate, but it was tainted. Whoever ate it would go mad. The grain would sustain life but would destroy sanity.

The king and his advisor thought and talked for days about what to do. They explored the possibility of finding enough food for the kingdom elsewhere, but they could not locate an adequate supply. Then they decided, for the good of the kingdom, they would simply keep for themselves the old supply of grain. That way, although everyone in the kingdom would be mad, they at least would be sane and able to manage the kingdom's affairs.

As they thought further on the matter, they came to a painful realization: In a kingdom where everyone is mad, and they alone sane, they would truly be the mad ones. How could they live in a world whose inhabitants were mad if they themselves were not?

They agonized night and day. At last they decided: They, too, would eat of the grain. They, too, would go mad. But they would put a mark on their foreheads so that when the two of them looked at each other, at least they would remember that they were mad.

Rabbi Nachman's story has many levels. Like many tormented, creative people, he felt he walked mad through the world, but, unlike others, he knew his own madness. Yet it is also the story about how we cannot know ourselves without another. Someone else is required to read and interpret the signs on our foreheads. *Einmal ist keinmal* is an old German saying—Once is not at all. Every experience requires repetition to become truly real. We might similarly say in understanding the self, One is nothing. The silhouette of one disappears in the horizon. When we lose ourselves, we must have others, others who are true. Sometimes the mirror reveals less of us than the window.

We fear losing ourselves in part because we are not sure there is something solid underneath. What if there is no solid "I" to return to? The philosopher David Hume claimed that as much as he searched for himself, all he could find were sensations, perceptions, but no fixed entity he could call "himself." Our roles and responses are so various, we feel confused about the reality of the self.

Confusion about who we are is rooted in our humanness. The poet Pablo Neruda wrote a poem called "We Are Many," in which he speaks about identifying so powerfully with different figures that he no longer knows who he is. At the movies, he identifies one moment with the cowboy, the next with the Indian. On watching a fire, sometimes he feels like the fireman, sometimes like the arsonist. He envies everything whole, certain, uncomplicated. He wishes he could study himself like he studies geography, and know where everything belongs and what it is called. As it is, he is full of contradictions, and the real Neruda escapes him.

Artists and writers speak of the power that flows through their fingers onto the canvas, or onto the page. The ancients expressed this feeling with muses: The muse came along and whispered in the artist's ear. In a less mythological age, we use the word "inspiration." It comes from the root "to breathe," and suggests that something passes through us, that something like breath comes from without and changes us within.

Inspiration might come from within and from beyond ourselves. We are subject to the currents of our souls and the tides of the universe. At times, we feel touched. Something enters us and mixes with the chemistry of our spirits. Emerson used to conceive of his writing self as a different person, to whom he even gave a name, because the quality of his inspiration when he sat down to compose his works was so different from what it was at other moments. Inspiration is not just an underground bubbling that swells up from some subterranean spring in the heart. Inspiration also sweeps in through the windows, airing out the soul, making us feel that we are receptors for great things. At such moments we feel as if the world and our own soul have suddenly begun to sing the same song.

We are, each of us, not disconnected beings but expressions of a universal flow whose direction we can express at special moments. Throughout their lives, human beings channel forces that are greater than themselves. The prophet is an extreme example of an individual who is the transmitter of forces beyond himself. The poet is another, and so too the dreamer. Dreams are pillaged for messages that lie not only deep inside but far outside our waking selves.

Such intuitions seem fleeting, however. The inspiration passes, and we return to the old division between ourselves and the world. It is frightening to be lost for more than a moment, to feel oneself dissolve before all that is greater. So our boundaries are resurrected, and once more we can say nothing greater than "I."

At first, what we are is called forth by others. My daughter watches me for clues. She finds out who she is by seeing how others respond. In time, her self will begin to be defined more by internal experience. She is discovering that who she is differs from her mother and father, and in that difference is the first space for her individuality. She is her own. If we are wise enough as parents to encourage without coercion, to set limits without fastening chains, she will soon realize that she shares her humanness and Divine spark with everyone, yet she is a copy of no one.

We are born originals, but still there are times when the self seems to slip away. The dehumanizing treatment we receive, and our own weaknesses, can rob us of our selves. The assigning of numbers to human beings is deliberately intended to strip them of their individual selves. The prisoner Jean Valjean in *Les Miserables* comes to think of himself as number 24601. The guards at the concentration camps during the Holocaust tattooed numbers on inmates' arms to convince them that they were not unique souls but a collection of numbers parading as selves. By shaving the prisoners' heads, forcing them to wear identical uniforms, and seeking to make everyone appear the same, they stripped the inmates of their selfhood. The only uniqueness the victims were allowed was the assigned number.

The Bible is preoccupied with the question of names. Adam's name comes from *adamah*, the earth, because he is formed from the ground. He then names the animals, thereby asserting his difference from them and mastery over them. Adam's name signifies his origin—dust. Eve's name (in Hebrew, Havvah) signifies her as the begetter of life.

So the original human beings tell us that what we are called is an integral part of who we are. And the Bible's fascination with names does not end there. Many of the most important characters mark shifts in their lives by changing their names.

Abram becomes Abraham. Sarai becomes Sarah. As each character begins to realize his or her full self, each assumes a new name. The most dramatic change is in Jacob, who, from his self-struggle, becomes Israel.

Moses' name is given to him by his adopted mother. It is significant that we do not know if he was given another name by his birth mother, or what it might have been. Moses is transformed from the start. Since he will grow up in the palace of the Pharaoh, he is destined for something different from his kindred. His self will be forged by the experience of rulership, not slavery.

Thus it is when Moses first encounters God, he requires a name. In Exodus 3:13, Moses claims that he needs to know God's name, for when the people ask him who it was that sent him, what can he say? God reveals the Divine appellation. Strangely, Moses does not repeat it to the people. The name is for Moses. He must know who this new and awesome being is that commands his allegiance. For Moses to find himself, he must understand the forces that act upon him. He cannot understand his own name without understanding God's.

Moses is not alone in this struggle. We, too, cannot understand who we are without some belief about the nature of the world. Since the self is intermixed with all things—Abram becomes Abraham in response to a call from God, Jacob becomes Israel in response to a struggle with an angel—we are constantly testing our own selves, our own names.

When my wife got her diagnosis of cancer, she began to think about her name. Her given name was Eileen. Yet Eileen is the one who got sick. Eileen is the one who did not know the lessons of sickness, because her life was lived before the cancer, which changed her into someone new. There is an old Jewish tradition of changing one's luck by changing one's name. She took her Hebrew name instead, and from Eileen she became Eliana.

At first the switch was difficult. When you have known someone with one name, the name has worn grooves in your tongue—it is hard for any other name to come out when you call the person. But in time, both the person and the name begin to shift. Now it is "Eliana," not "Eileen," whom I married, who is the mother of our daughter, who fought cancer and guards against its recurrence. Eileen is the name she was given. Eliana is the name she earned, the name that is truly hers. Eliana means "God has answered."

Moses needs God's name to understand his own. Similarly, the crisis of cancer brought Eliana face-to-face with God and helped her to her true name. It was a process accelerated by crisis. When the world forces us to ask who we are, why we want to live, who we want to be, we are confronted by our names. Our roles are in question—am I now a husband, a father, a rabbi, a writer, a friend, all of those, none? What name do I wear when I speak with this person, with that one? Why did Moses keep the name given to him by his adopted mother? Perhaps he wished to prove that he was worthy of having been saved from the river.

We move through our lives gaining roles and acquiring

names, but also losing them. Every choice, every name, every role is a turning away from another possibility. Every name is a possibility and a limitation. As we create, we also leave behind. It is faith in the importance of our ultimate mission, and our ultimate worth, that allows us to reinvent ourselves by creating and finding who we are.

Whether and how we are lost depend upon how we react to our world. Some situations that we put ourselves in obscure who we are, and some reveal. Two people win the lottery. One person drowns in the wealth and it destroys his life. Another becomes a philanthropist and it enriches his life. The money did not create character but revealed it. Parts of the self that might have been hidden were suddenly seen. I know a man who was a petty thief. He was addicted to drugs and alcohol. In the end he went to prison. In prison he met all sorts of people. He began to think of the ways in which he measured his life against the people he met there. He saw things in them that lived in him as well. He saw people of goodness and talent who did not have the strength to renounce the pieces of themselves that left them morally crippled. He told me about a man he met who was a mathematical genius but who had never used his phenomenal talent for anything other than swindles. The thrill of quick money, of outsmarting systems, was too great for him to renounce. He understood that the self has to be whittled away at, that parts of it have to be discarded in order for us to create a self that is worthy of the gifts we have been given. When he left prison, he changed his life.

He noticed that in prison, many people reexplored their faith. There were a lot of reasons why, but the one that motivated him was to find a way out of himself. But now he realized, he told me, that he needed a way into himself, into the part of himself that could live worthily in the world. Today he is a rabbi. Pieces of "rabbi" were always in him, waiting to be assembled. Had he not first been lost, he would not have found himself.

People lose themselves in far less extreme circumstances as well. I have two photographs taken of myself as a child at about the same age—roughly seven or eight. One is for a school picture. I look carefully put together, with matching shirt and sweater (no doubt I was specially dressed for the occasion). My hair is combed, and I have on the self-conscious half-smile that betrays unease. The other photograph is black and white. I seem thoughtful, somber. I look at the two together and think, *Mask and face*. One is real, one a pose. Children of clergy are not so different from the children of politicians or other figures who are constantly judged by their constituents. When I was a child, the community let me know it had an investment in me—how I dressed, what I thought, how I behaved, whether I achieved. I think the school picture is the part of me that liked the attention. My brothers and I were special. Or at least we were treated as special. The unease in the smile is my uncertainty about whether I was doing it right.

Part of the distance I see in the second photo is the distance of someone whose self is hidden away.

Looking at those photographs of myself as a child, I ask: What would the child I was think of the adult I have become? How stark has the transformation been from child to adult? Would I seem sincere, or plastic? Would my tricks of ingratiation work with that child, or would they seem simple and phony? I cannot know, because that child, both sides of him, are far away.

We have passed through the vogue of reclaiming our inner child. For all the rhetoric about recovering the children who dwell at some incomprehensible reserve within us, once we pass a certain stage in life, we are different, and part of ourselves is lost at each point in the passage. The self is still there, but the butterfly cannot be spun back into the cocoon. In films and fairy tales alone does the arrow of time turn back.

That child, the one who looks out at me from a small black-and-white snapshot, is gone. I recognize, by act of imagination, my own eyes in his. I connect with him as a form of what I once was. His slightly haunted look makes me wonder at the sadness I harbored then that has vanished, or has perhaps left a mark in my psyche likes stripes in a sea shell. Is that a self I can no longer reach? Or has it simply dissolved into the larger guise of adulthood?

Another image: When I see each of these photographs, I think maybe we are Russian dolls, with selves built like smooth tops fitting one in the other. The one beneath is never entirely lost, not really, but it is swallowed as part of the self that is layered over it. We cannot peel off the outer selves. But each of our selves is there, like one civilization built atop the other, and each takes from the one beneath. Sometimes what we take helps us; sometimes it hinders us.

So we are a succession of selves. Each self is somehow a contination of what went before. Yet it is also not the same. Anyone who has kept a diary, a journal, or any record of early years knows how much of a stranger we can feel to the selves of earlier days. Once or twice in my life I kept a journal. The voice is recognizably mine. Still it is more frantic, worried about issues and people that I have long forgotten. I read from sentence to sentence, alternating between "Is this me?" and "Yes, this is me."

Old selves embarrass us, but we also miss them. No matter how we have grown, what we were retains an unrecoverable magic. In the cavern of memory, there is an echo of what we were. But we are no longer in that place; our way is barred. The portals swing one way, and we peer back at a world whose sensations are recoverable only by our fading, hazy memories and the tenuous magic of art.

We lose not only our selves but the parts of the world where that self was a reality. We were in a certain context; we were in this neighborhood, under these trees, beside this brook, attending this school. When we return, they are not, they cannot be, the same. The ache of loss runs through our hearts and pours out onto the world.

There is an ebb and flow to the self. At times we are strong; at other times we totter. A mysterious psychic tide wells up in us, then abates. We all are children of the tides in this special sense. In the course of our lives, our vigor waxes and wanes, our faith is uneven, our fulfillment various.

The process of self-loss intensifies as we grow older. Age is a thief. Gradually it steals things we considered a birthright. When I talk with older people, one of the recurrent themes I hear is that healthy youth cannot imagine the creeping decline, the scattershot way aging puts pain in one's bones and sinews. The world of objects can become a world of obstacles, as climbing stairs and twisting jar lids change from automatic operations to reminders of the diminished ease and amplitude of one's limbs.

Any sensitive young person feels the frustration of older people who seek to explain that age is inconceivable. Before one's eyes stands a gray-haired, wizened woman insisting she cannot imagine that she is really eighty-five years old. Old age operates like the demise of a long relationship; even though we see it coming and watch its progress, its onset catches us by surprise.

Is the gain of wisdom real? Would we do things differently knowing what we know now? Or would the passions of youth again overmaster our sense? Would we live wiser, or does wisdom really consist of the ability to give others wise counsel that they, in turn, may disregard as we did?

The losses of age often deepen our sense of regret. Looking back over a lifetime, one sees that there are possibilities that were never realized. In youth, there seemed still the chance that those possibilities might be fulfilled. My father is breaking apart his considerable library. Every few weeks I receive a shipment of books, books that I have associated with him all my life. It is unsettling to think of them as mine. When he first discussed with me and my brothers distributing the library, he said to us, "What is so strange is that these books have been so dear to me, and now I know most of them I will never reread." Perhaps if he had 100 years, he still would not reread them, but he could live with the freshness of the possibility.

Age, like all losses, seems to present us with the possibility of making loss meaningful. In a wry way that is the theme of the song from Learner and Loewe's *Gigi*—"I'm glad that I'm not young anymore." The song is the older man's way of saying that the waning of youth's passions, its frivolities, opens the way for him to live more deliberately and serenely. Whether he would really take youth back were it offered does not even matter, for it is not a choice. The question is whether he will fashion something meaningful from his losses. Will he let the universe defeat him, or will he use loss by turning its own force to his advantage?

God created man in his image. In the image of God He created him" (Gen. 1:27).

For most of biblical history, this verse was taken as a tautology—the first half of the verse and the second were understood to express the same thought, that the human being was created in the image of God. But the Kotzker Rebbe saw the verse as expressing two different ideas. The first half, he said, means that each individual is created in that individual's own image. Then we receive the infusion of the Divine spark. In other words, our own uniqueness comes first. We are stamped with the image that will be only ours, and then we receive an ember of God.

The building block of life is our own singularity. Although we all are human beings, all are kin, and all are mandated to build community, we are also specially stamped. The grain in each human character shows whorls and textures as unique as a fingerprint.

Human beings are uniquely valuable precisely because of their uniqueness. But how many people realize their uniqueness? How many are prepared to aid others in doing the same? There is a lovely legend about the angels' objection to God's creation of human beings. Why would God insist upon placing a Divine spark in the human world when its only proper place is in heaven? Finally the angels and God reach a compromise. God will place the Divine spark in the world below, but the angels can hide it wherever they like, to conceal it from human beings. The angels think and search. They know that eventually human beings will search to the bottom of the sea and atop the highest mountain, so the spark should not be placed there. Where is the only place people will not look? Finally they know—they tell God to place it inside the human heart.

In each human being is a dignity that is often betrayed through indolence or neglect. We fail to realize who we are and who we should be. There are some people, prophets, certain artists, who always seem to know for what they were destined. For most of us the effort is to push our souls up the hill until we reach the vista we were intended to survey.

So we stop at places in the journey and pretend that is where we should be. A man takes a job at thirty, and he has visions of something better. In time, routine throws a blanket over his hopes, and he sleeps dreamlessly for the next thirty years. He has not so much abandoned his dreams as forgotten his self.

To continue searching takes energy, and it takes courage. We do not know what will happen if we refuse to rest. Perhaps our lives will have to turn around. Perhaps we will have to give up something that makes us comfortable. Certainly no block in the soul is more potent than fear. Fear is the combatant in the life battle, presenting itself in all sorts of disguises. Stories of great achievement are almost always founded on the overcoming of fear. Courage is not a quality limited to battlefields. Courage is the test of everyday. Failures of honesty are usually failures of courage.

The Kotzker Rebbe, whose profound emphasis on the uniqueness of each human being we have already witnessed, often intimidated his disciples. His rigor and his anger frightened them. But that was not his desire. He wanted to raise disciples who would have the strength that he had, to stand as he did, to be individuated—who they really were. Like all true teachers, he wished for them to stand up to the light in themselves. Once, in exasperation, he screamed at his disciples: "Masks! Where are your faces?"

Inward goes the way full of mystery," wrote the poet and mystic Novalis. We do not expect, when we are honest, where we will end up. Inside of us is a pageant of mystery.

In my own life I have done a succession of things I was sure I would never do. Early in life I decided the rabbinate would never be for me. Later I decided that although I would enter the rabbinate, I would write, lecture, and teach—as I did for the first ten years of my career—but never become the rabbi of a synagogue. Then I became the rabbi of a synagogue. In succession, I am forced to question the contours of this "I" I thought I knew so well. As I watch myself losing some of the characteristics I believed were mine, I come to know myself better. Or rather, I come to watch what shape I now have taken. I am uncovering and creating "I." We chip away at the block of stone, and there are many possible sculptures underneath.

Religious traditions praise humility. The praise is simpleminded if all it means is that one should not be arrogant. But it means much more than that. It means recognizing for a moment that one is nothing. We are, as one physicist put it, the ashes of dead stars. Our selves are bits that once swirled about the universe and will again long after we are gone. Our egos, which loom so large, are literally nothing, no-thing.

To know that, to feel it, is not demeaning. For on the heels of that recognition is everything we are. We are unique but not independent. The dissolving of ego lets us see the true reality of others and gives us back our selves. When you are nothing, you do not need to prop yourself up with artificial rigging to ensure you stay afloat.

Saul was lost because he did not believe deeply enough in his core. The more he was elevated in life, the more insecure he became. He looked for threats from without. He saw his own fate as being decided by David, by Samuel, by God. He might have been saved had he been wise enough to realize that both his anguish and his answer were within.

The Kotzker Rebbe once greeted a young man who had come to the small town of Kotzk to study with him.

"Why did you come to Kotzk?"

"I came," said the young man, "to learn."

"No," said the rebbe," you can learn elsewhere. Why did you come to Kotzk?"

"I came," said the young man, "to find God."

"No," said the rebbe, "you can find God everywhere. God does not live only in Kotzk. Once more, why did you come to Kotzk?"

The student, frustrated and anxious, said, "I do not know, Rebbe. Why did I come to Kotzk?"

"You came to Kotzk to find yourself."

At that moment, perhaps the student realized that the answers to his other questions, about knowledge, about God, about fate, would be bound up in his understanding of himself. Although no picture exists of the Kotzker Rebbe, I like to think that at that moment in his eyes was not only a characteristic fierceness but also playfulness, even love.

If we wish to know who we are, we must watch ourselves, explore ourselves, remember ourselves, release ourselves. We must fill ourselves up with the gains and losses of love.

Five

Love

The elegy of loss begins in fall and reaches its most plaintive notes in winter. The cycle of seasons symbolizes the eternal human movement from having to losing. Green to brown, sprig to sear, each moment of life is tinged with loss.

Love prefigures loss. Softly at first, then roaringly, love whispers its own inevitable absence. Small separations nudge the veil aside and remind us of the day when our beloved will be gone. Between the embrace and the parting is the chronicle of love. Togetherness is filled with looks that prophesy absence, glimpses or imaginings of futures when one shall be alone. Love is an ever fixed mark in the minds of poets, but in the world, love can fade or end. "Love alters not with his brief hours and weeks," wrote Shakespeare, "but bears it out even to the edge of doom." We want to believe it. But for those who have lost love, the heroic words about everlastingness are mocked by the pain of unhealed hearts.

The curtain closes over the lovers of movies or plays after they have overcome obstacles and been reunited. But could we see further into their lives, if love extended beyond clearing the props and extinguishing the stage lights, we would see the weary duties of every day begin to drag down the lovers of youth. The dashing romantic hero becomes a restless middle-aged man, dissatisfied with a life so different from his occasional, still fevered dreams. The lovely, dewy woman of the first act becomes a harried partner who wants to be caressed and cherished, but her life feels empty of the ardent devotion promised.

I spend time talking to engaged couples not only about their wedding ceremonies but also about their lives and their love. Older couples, those who are not marrying for the first time, are sometimes more passionate about each other but, behind the passion, also more frightened. They have seen that forever can be an illusion, that death, or the distance that grows with years, has dissolved what they once had. Believing that this time is for sure, they do not have the luxury of no doubts. As one man said to me, away from the hearing of his fiancée: "I love her very much, and I am going to be with her forever." He paused for a moment and sighed. "I said that once before, didn't I?"

In the movie *Ghost*, Patrick Swayze, whose character has been killed, manages to reappear and contact his love, Demi Moore. At the very end, when the murder has been solved and they have seen each other again for a gauzy moment, Swayze ascends to heaven. Many people I know left the movie very touched by the love story. But I kept thinking, I pity her next boyfriend. After all, she is still on earth, and her next beau has to compete with the image of an angelic dead lover. That was, in a nutshell, the predicament the movie left the moviegoers in as well. We were fed an eternal ideal, but we lead real lives.

These realities of shared life do not make the movie. The losses we endure through the years may not be marketable, but they are inseparable from love. The early Greek philosopher Heraclitus told us that we cannot step into the same river twice. The swift current will always remake the river; nothing stays the same. Love adores the rushing river because it believes itself the one fixed point in a swirling universe. How painful to discover that it, too, changes.

The inescapable paradox of love is this: It is made precious by time, which threatens to destroy it. Only through loss can we love, but it is loss that wracks our hearts.

Men and women who have lost their spouses struggle with this dilemma. Of course, the years are worth the hurt, I am told, but the hurt is so great. How can I sleep alone in a bed after forty years? Eat breakfast by myself? Have no one to whom I can tell the small incidents of my day? Rabbi, part of me believes it would be better never to love. Each morning I wake up expecting him to be there. I cannot bear the thought of how many lonely mornings there are to come. The world is empty.

The great love stories of the Western tradition, Romeo and Juliet, Tristan and Isolde, Heloise and Abelard, are stories of love snatched away by fate, by wickedness, by death. Filled with evil families and magic potions, these tales have gripped us for centuries. Their plots are replayed, with different backdrops and names, each day across the globe in music, movies, television, theater. The story recurs because it is love's eternal tale: that which is beautiful and doomed. Each of these renowned love stories is a tragedy, because love is a bloom straining toward eternity, but it is planted in the soil of impermanence.

Adam and Eve do not love each other in the garden. The garden is forever. Although they are together, the text does not relate a single act of love. It is only in the wake of exile, when death looms, that "Adam knew his wife Eve" (Gen. 4:1). Intimacy is our protest against mortality. Created together, each needs the other to feel whole again in the land where there is death.

Love is a fierce clinging in the face of fate. That is why it languishes in an eternal, perfect Eden. Love blooms only where leaves fall.

What is the meaning of this pageant of love and loss? Why are we drawn to tragic tales of love, from ancient times to modern movies? Few things in life are judged by the absolute standard of love. Love, it seems, must last forever to be thought a success. Love that ends is so fraught with pain that it is hard to think of it untinged by the pain of its ending. Only lasting love seems true; that is why the movies end before love fades.

The current wisdom reinforces the assumptions of the romantic age, but we have made the test of love harder by unsentimental science. We have learned that biology fights against faithfulness, too. We are not programmed for monogamy, but faithfulness is still the great measure of a life. All at once, society holds both conceptions of love: On the one hand, it is a trick of biology, a stratagem of the life force; on the other hand, we elevate the emotion to a centerpiece of life, the muse of poetry and song, the true raison d'être of our brief span on earth.

Loss of love is so painful because love is not an episode; it is the aim. If love is fleeting, the whole enterprise seems unworthy.

The great expression of love in the Bible is the Song of Songs. This magnificent love poem gives lyrical expression to love yoked to longing: "You have captured my heart, my own, my bride. You have captured my heart with one glance of your eyes. I was asleep, but my heart was wakeful. Hark, my beloved knocks. Let me in, my own, my darling . . ." (4:9, 5:2).

But the central expression of the Song of Songs is found in its most quoted line: "Love is as strong as death" (8:6). As strong as death, but no stronger. A romantic might take issue with this statement and urge that love is eternal. Love poetry has traditionally celebrated this solidity of love. Love will outlast monuments, even suns and stars.

We wish for a love that will last. For love is the shield against loneliness. Loneliness haunts us throughout human life, and love is the great weapon we wield against it. But for love to endure, it must be more than love. True love is an outgrowth of the ability to have faith.

Love itself is an act of faith. Our mistake is to believe that it is an act of faith in the beloved. Surely faith in the beloved is part of it, but deeper is faith in the world, and in the presiding Spirit of the world. When we love, we have faith that this universe will be kind to love, believes in it with us, will enable it to grow. Through faith, love is granted its measure of immortality. Fragile creatures cling to one another. We are buffeted by misfortune. Faith crosses the bridge of longing, the gulf of loss.

Love never ends with the beloved.

Once I spoke to a couple, both of whom had endured a great deal—sickness, loss, financial difficulties. When I asked him what he loved about her, he strung together superlatives about her character, her beauty, her goodness. I asked her. "Rabbi, when I am with him, despite all I have gone through, I trust in the world," she said.

Romantic love, with its accents of deep, unquenchable passion and longing, is not entirely about the beloved. Stendahl, the great French novelist, wrote a book called *On Love*, in which he explores romantic love and compares the process to the crystallization that happens in the salt mines of Salzburg. If a twig is left in the salt mines, eventually an encrustation develops. Intricate patterns of salt make the simple twig quite beautiful. The same thing happens, says Stendahl, when we fall passionately in love. The magnificence we see is not entirely the being of the other person. It is our own longing surrounding the beloved with a matrix of beauty.

Love is one of the ways we grope toward God. Amid all our doubts and wonderment, there is another person in the world whose spirit catches our own. Her eyes sparkle, and something makes us feel suddenly alive, alive on a more vivid plane than we were the moment before. The change is in us and in the world. The marvels we have heard of now live in us. The rudderless world suddenly seems fashioned by a Spirit whose hand is that of an artist. Love has lent us faith.

When I was in rabbinical school, a couple I knew split up. He was a rabbinical student, and they had been together for years. After the breakup, he began to question not so much his judgment but his faith. Where was the order of the world that he had staked his life on if such a thing could happen? Love was his surety that the world operated correctly. Now, by love having slipped away, God seemed to have become indifferent to him.

One late night, we had a conversation and he told me about his pain. Since I was not then in love, I listened as an outsider, a land dweller hearing about someone stranded at sea. He contemplated leaving rabbinical school because he could not convey love for a God whose world was so bereft of love. I tried to assure him that in his life, love might be like the tide, that it would return. He said he realized that, but knowing its fragility, could he feel as secure in his faith again?

The crisis was real and lasted for more than a year. After the year, he fell in love again. His faith returned. But now it was based on a more fearful trust.

Love can begin with God's absence. One of the reasons why love has grown to be so important in modern literature and myth is that the competing passion of people's lives, the passion for God, has waned. Where do we draw upon the powers of passion and devotion inside of ourselves if we cannot turn them to the heavens? We turn them to the beloved. In the stunning phrase of Jose Luis Borges: "To fall in love is to create a religion with a fallible god." We create that fallible god.

In the absence of something greater than the lovers, the world does not conspire in their love. They love in a void. The two spirits have nowhere to look but to each other. They have nowhere to turn *together*. They can gaze into each other's eyes, but they cannot stand shoulder to shoulder and look in the same direction, for it seems nothing in the world is equal to the intensity of their love. So the love focuses inward.

Loving in a faith-filled world begins with the swelling of

feeling inside. As love grows, we discover a new palette of internal colors and know anew how kaleidoscopic is our inner world. Love tinged with faith breaks us free of the constraints and smallness of our world. Suddenly we are as enlarged as the horizon.

Such a feeling is how classical mystics spoke about their feeling for God. They were expanded in their love for the Divine. Boundaries fell away.

This intersection of faith and love may explain why mystical literature in every religion is filled with sexual imagery. The first time I fell in love, the world grew more magical. I could not sleep at night. I seemed to be part of some giant understanding about the goodness and beauty of the world. The pains of the love were not just a small incident but the world turning against me. Each step of love said something about the world. Like my friend in later years in rabbinical school, I felt that being in love was a declaration of the world's meaning.

It was seventh grade. In tandem, I was developing romantic interests and intellectual interests. So while I was deciding that the world was cold, run by scientific principles, and that religion was a daydream, I was also celebrating the rushing wonder of being in love. The splendor of that sensation challenged my icy view of reality. Maybe some of the truth lay in what I experienced, not what I knew. I would argue that the world was indifferent, and all the while I could not wait to get to school. On an infinitely higher level, religious mysticism teaches us how our motivations have parallels in the structure of the world. Though mysticism can be quite intricate and intellectually demanding, it pays homage to how we feel, not only what we know. Love is more than what goes on inside us. According to the great mystics, love flows back and forth throughout the channels of creation.

By linking love and faith I do not mean that God manages our romantic lives. I have my doubts that God conveniently arranges loves to walk across the horizon of our lives at moments when we need them. The process seems far more haphazard than that. The challenge arises for us to lose love without losing faith. Sometimes the pain is so great that it persuades us to give up not just on love but on the world. Losing love often leads to depression, which is itself an indication of the abandonment of faith because of anger, or of pain. Depression is a turning inward because the world outside no longer seems charged with value and meaning. No one, however close, can penetrate the depressed person's shell of distance, at least not for a while.

Suddenly life seems empty or worthless. Why should I get dressed, talk to friends, read a book, see a movie, smile? These things are empty. Indeed, they are—in a world that is dulled, everything inside seems gray, cheerless. Depression is a global collapse of faith.

Once a man came to see me who had written me a heartwrenching letter. He was almost unable to function; nothing he did seemed important or rewarding. After his girlfriend broke up with him, he slid into a deep depression. His parents were frantic, and finally angry that he would not "pull himself together" and find some useful way to spend his days. He had been well educated, and yet now was flitting from field to field, resting nowhere, finding meaning in nothing.

He sat on the couch in my office, sullen, resigned. He permitted the rejection to define his identity and his worth. He was

the lost guy who had been dumped. Time and the encourage-
ment of others helped him recognize that her judgment need
not be his, and that love was wider than the love that had been
lost.

The key issue in loss of love is the knowledge that one did
love, and can love again. When my first love, mostly unrequited,
finally was dashed, it was this thought that gave me whatever
solace I had. It could not be that there is no one else to love.
The world is too full, my heart is too willing.

I look back on that time now as a time of real faith. Although
I was at a stage in life when I did not believe in God, I was not
faithless. I trusted the world.

Even the loss of the beloved is finally a part of a larger mosaic
of meaning.

In the book of Proverbs, we find the disturbing statement "For
whom the Lord loves, he rebukes" (3:12). The Talmudic sage
rabbi Akiva, seeking to explain why good people suffer so,
developed from this verse the idea that suffering is a mark of dis-
tinctive love from God. When someone suffers, there are a few
possibilities. Perhaps there is no God, and the world is a carni-
val of the absurd. Rabbi Akiva could not believe this possibility.
Perhaps there is a God, but God is not good or kind. But Akiva,
both by tradition and by his sense of the world, was convinced
that we are the products of a benevolent God. He was sure that
the Spirit that infuses the universe is beautiful, wondrous, compassionate. There are then two more possibilities: God is angry
at the misdeeds of human beings, or somehow chastisements are
bound up with love. This explanation is counterintuitive at best,

grotesque at worst. Can it be true that being loved is any kind of reward for having suffered?

Yet Akiva's point is twofold. He was a clear-eyed appraiser of the world. Living 2,000 years ago, Akiva did not deceive himself; he knew that the world is filled with suffering. He may not have known the story of the mustard seed, but it would not have surprised him. The story is about a man who loses his wife. He is devastated and seeks comfort. He travels to an old woman in the village who, he has heard, holds the answers to life's great questions. He tells her of his loss and his pain.

The woman sits quietly, listening to the travail of the bereaved husband. Then she responds, "There is a plant that can cure the pain of loss. But it must be specially grown. In order to grow it, you must find a mustard seed from a home that has known no loss."

The man sets out eagerly on his quest. He soon discovers that each home he approaches has a tale of woe. He returns to the woman and says, "Now I understand. There is no home without loss." The woman smiles gently.

Akiva knew that suffering is inevitable in this world, and he believed that suffering is part of the testing and refining process of life. The gravity and authority of the sufferer are clear to others. When we hear someone speak who has endured great suffering, we feel the power in his words. Pain helps shape wisdom. The sufferer who has triumphed over suffering is an aristocrat of the soul. We feel that the sufferer is the one who has been there and has drawn the lessons.

For Rabbi Akiva, those who are especially dear to God are expected to survive and surmount more than others. They are granted the gift of greater burdens. The treasured child is more freighted with expectations. But the expectations are not enough. To feel pain is not automatically ennobling. God may grant burdens, but only human beings can decide if they will use the losses of life to grow or to be embittered.

This first interpretation is difficult enough. We know how problematic it can be to be a favored child, and how much suffering it can entail. The philosopher John Stuart Mill wrote a remarkable autobiography that chronicles his unique childhood. His accomplishments as a young prodigy are astonishing—he learned classical languages at three, and read difficult, intricate books at age five. But we are unsurprised that he suffered a breakdown at twenty, and recovered by reading poetry and rediscovering nature. The expectations of parents may bring the sufferings of love, but they can be crushing. In the modern world, we are likely to expect God to be a more skilled parent. Nonetheless, Mill went on to become an important philosopher. Would he have changed his life if he could? Was his father's demanding love ultimately to his benefit or detriment?

When I was teaching at a seminary, I counseled a young man from a very accomplished family. From childhood there were great expectations placed upon him. He was expected to succeed. He did, for a while. In time the press of expectations became too much, and he wanted to escape. Rather than pursue a career, he wanted to find a quiet place, and a quiet life, to reflect and grow. His parents sent him to me, assuming that I would somehow persuade him to accept their views of him and of the world.

He had a gentle demeanor and tired eyes. We soon discovered that we shared a syndrome—neither of us had very clear memories of our childhoods. He asked me why I thought that was so. I answered honestly. First, I said that I have a very weak personal memory, and always have. I often forget conversations, faces, encounters that I wish to remember. My forgetfulness about childhood is also, I believe, a product of special circumstances—throughout much of my childhood, I felt the need to present myself a certain way. I was part of a public family, and I felt that my parents, even my community, were judged partly on how I behaved. So I tried to be what I assumed I should be, and not always what I was. I hid inside myself. I don't remember my childhood at least in part because I wasn't there for it.

He smiled and eagerly agreed. Yes, he too felt as though he had hidden. He knew that now, although he was an adult, his parents had not changed the rules. The same things were expected of him, but he could not hide anymore. He did not value many of the things he was encouraged to value. He suffered for the expectations, even though he believed them to be expectations of love.

His depressions had deepened. His parents' solution was for him to "do something." They thought that his depression originated in the waste of his powers. Since he was not exercising his talents, he was depressed. But he believed that the depression was a sickness of his soul.

Some might say that this child's parents did not love him if they had expectations. But they believed him capable of great things, and they placed the burdens of the favored child on his shoulders. What if in running away he was betraying his talent, and would one day regret it? The sufferings of love run both ways. Rabbi Akiva too felt that God suffers when we betray our possibilities.

In time, this young man did succeed, but not as his parents wished. After urging him to keep a journal, I watched him progress as a writer. He never became the successful businessman his parents had expected. He did not lose their love, but he felt their disappointment. He still feels it, and it fuels his writing.

Greek myths suggested to Freud that people suffer from an Oedipus complex. A careful reading of the Bible suggests that people suffer also from an Isaac complex. The Oedipal complex deals (in part) with the urge of children to destroy their parents. The Bible reverses the paradigm: It tells of how parents sometimes destroy their children. We have seen it enacted in the story of the binding of Isaac, and in Saul's behavior toward David as a surrogate father. It is present in a horrendous tale told in the book of Judges (chapter 11), in which a wild chieftain named Yiftach actually sacrifices his own daughter. Even in the Joseph story, there is a hint of the desire to do away with one's offspring. Jacob loves his child Joseph, but love does not preclude destructive impulses. It is Jacob who—although aware of the brothers' jealousy—sends Joseph off to check on his brothers, thus setting up the situation to enact a riveting drama and a near fatal tragedy.

How love wraps itself about loss is the leitmotif of the story of Joseph. Joseph's brothers originally intend to kill him. In the end, he is sold by his brothers into slavery because he is the special object of his father's love. Love and consequent hatred lead to the loss of all Joseph knows. In Egypt he manages briefly to succeed. He becomes the steward of a powerful man. Then his master's wife conceives a passionate desire for him, and his attempts to escape her land him in jail. Joseph is victimized by the love he arouses in others.

The Midrash tells a story highlighting Joseph's dilemma: "A man once said to Joseph: 'I love you very much,' to which Joseph replied: 'Love has caused me great suffering; my father's love brought upon me my brethren's hatred, which resulted in my being sold as a slave; the love of Potiphar's wife lodged me in prison.' " Here is Akiva's insight made flesh—sometimes love is the bearer of pain.

Loving itself is often the cause of loss. I first began to understand this paradox in high school. I pushed away the girls I had crushes on by giving them unwanted attention. Those whom I did not care so much about were far more likely to be drawn to me, because I treated them with an equanimity that invited interest. The effort to be insouciant, to be casual, with those whose attention I really craved was constant. But the eagerness always shone through. During our teenage years, attention is often counterproductive. The lesson changes in adulthood, although not that much. When love is too insistent, it often pushes the beloved away. We do not aid love by depriving it of oxygen. In desire there must be a trace of nonchalance; wanting must be kept alive, and it is stifled by too much having.

Pain is certainly indispensable to romantic love. Angst is the potent spice that makes the dish almost unbearable, and therefore irresistible. In Turgenev's brief novel *First Love*, the older but wiser narrator comments, "I say that my passion began from that day; and I might add that my suffering began on that day too," and later, "I cannot even begin to convey the feelings with which I left her. I never wish to experience them again, but I should count it a misfortune never to have had them at all." The object of his love, Zinaida, suffers at the end as well. Few plays, ancient or modern, could carry a plot without the anguish that love evokes. Judicious love, measuring-spoon love that never exceeds or overdemands, love that is reasonable and manageable—such love is not love. It is a tempered folly, a sedate affection. Love may not always be the wild, frantic swoon of the romantics, but it cannot be cool, professorial, wearing patched sleeves and oval glasses, peering discriminatingly at the beloved, calculating exact dimensions of emotion and intention. Love is not the antithesis of reason, but neither is it its kin.

We love some things in this world without desire. We can love the mountains, but we do not desire to possess them. We can love the stars without wishing to own the galaxy. There is a nobility to disinterested love. It is a miserly soul that loves only that which can be owned or consumed. Nonetheless, we can lose that which we do not have. We do not own the world, but in death, we lose it. There may be love without possession, but there is no love without loss.

To love is to accept the possibility of suffering. The day our daughter was born, my wife and I accepted a new level of suffering into our lives, because being a parent demands a new kind of love. Before Samara was born, I did not know what it was to hear a child cry and not be able to make the situation right. I did not know what it was to feel that most keen, pointed pain of not always being able to protect one's child. They are sufferings of love, brutal sufferings at times, that can be avoided only by not loving. Human beings continue to have children because beyond the fear, there is still faith: the faith that the world into which we brought our daughter is worthy; the faith that even when we no longer can stand with her, she will never be alone.

Nonetheless, the world sometimes demands that love be measured against other needs. The parent who goes off to work in the morning, leaving children at home or in day care, balances competing needs and loves. The writer who believes he has something to say, and removes himself from his family for several hours to tap on a computer or scratch on a pad, balances competing loves. Loss is not less real because we choose it.

I once officiated at a funeral for a woman who had lived a good, long life. Her daughter, an only child, told me a lovely story about her. They lived in Chicago, and mother and daughter were very close. As the time came for her to go to college, the daughter happened to take a trip out West. She became enamored of Stanford. Her mother was extremely upset. The prospect of losing her only child (it was before air travel was easy or common) filled her with sadness and even dread.

The mother went out to see the school anyway. On the trip home to Chicago, she read Margaret Mead's autobiography and learned that the famed anthropologist had a daughter who required all sorts of special education. Mead was tireless in seeking to provide her daughter with what she needed. When this woman landed, she immediately told her daughter, "You don't have to worry, sweetheart. I read about how much Mead sacrificed for her daughter. Then I thought of you, with all your promise, all you have to give to the world. I realized I had no right to hold you back. If Stanford is what you wish, that is where you will go." Her loss was no less great for the nobility of her love.

Such selflessness reflects a rare willingness to change. More often, part of us will change in reaction to the other, but we tend to keep intact the deepest parts of ourselves. When the medieval monarch Charlemagne marched the Saxon soldiers through the Rhine river to baptize them, the soldiers kept their right arms aloft, out of the river—because that was the arm they fought with, and they did not want to change that. They were willing to change everything but the essential part of themselves, the part they treasured.

Often in relationships we keep our sword arms aloft. We will change everything but what counts in our lives. We will adjust, but not too much. We will change only if the changes do not discomfit us.

My father once gave my brother some wise advice right before his marriage. He said, whatever bothers you about your fiancée, it will get worse. Do not marry someone in order to change them. Marry someone whose flaws you can live with. For part of our vanity is that another's flaws are irritating and our own are harmless.

I have seen marriages dissolve over one partner's denial that his or her behavior has consequences for the other. The husband says, "She doesn't really mind that I spend all day watching TV," and all the while the wife is pleading for the recognition that she *does* really mind.

When we first fall in love, nothing else seems to matter. But over time, the relationship transforms, and what was certain and clear becomes dizzyingly confused. We have given away pieces of ourselves in order to love. In time, old interests and passions reemerge, and we wonder if what we abandoned was more valuable than we thought at the time. Maybe I should not have sacrificed this career, or that interest, or another connection.

Some of my contemporaries question their own wishes to

give their lives to another, to children, or to love. They hear their married friends express certain regrets over opportunities lost.

In my work with singles, I speak to people who are determined to remain alone. Another person will encumber their freedom. Some will marry but not have children, because they feel that their life's work makes them unsuitable as parents. They see their parents' lives and do not want to be in the same situation or, as one person put it, caught in the same trap.

The trap, if there is one, is that love itself precludes other love. Once we have committed to one person, the desire for others is not automatically erased. We meet other people whose charms are evident, with whom we feel an instant kinship. Perhaps there too is the promise of love. But the inability to resist that will result in wounding or destroying the initial love. Again the questing heart runs up against the first law of loss, which is that we are here for a limited time on earth, we cannot have all that we want, and choosing anything means losing something else.

It is hard. It does not seem fair. We should be able to love freely. But to love freely, ultimately, means that we cannot love deeply and for a lifetime.

Romantic myths teach us that for each heart in this world, there is but one other heart. The idea of destined lovers finding each other is a powerful one. In my experience, our lives can take different directions depending upon whom we choose, and the possibilities for love are many. We are many people inside, and we are not unitary in our responses. We are drawn to this one's goodness, that one's charm, another's tenderness. Since our lives are limited, however, and since fidelity is the spine of love that lasts, we foreclose other possibilities of love. We lose love in order to be able to love.

Faith is what makes the loss bearable. The lover has faith not that a single heart beats out there, but that his own heart is wide enough, capacious enough to find someone to love. There were times in my life when I thought it impossible that someone would love me—or someone whom I loved would love me. When I doubted most strongly, when the thought depressed me, I felt a general lack of faith in the world and its governance. When I could shore up my faith that this world was not arbitrary, not ultimately purposeless but worthy, then I could believe that love would come.

College was the time in my life when my friends and I talked endlessly about love—if it was real, if it would come into our lives, how we would find it, what it would be like, what sorts of people we would find to love. I remember having these discussions with one friend in particular. They began philosophically and always ended personally. But we were talking not only about love, although we thought love was our sole subject. We were talking about a life that mattered. Would we find our ways to usefulness, to blessing, even, to being a part of something greater than ourselves? As William James wrote, "The great use of life is to spend it for something that will outlast it." We were hoping not only for someone to love but for something to last.

In college I made endless resolutions about myself that never seemed to be realized. I would be less self-conscious, more aware of myself; more serious, less serious; less at the whim of my impulses, more spontaneous. That the resolutions contradicted each other mattered less than that I always seemed to come out myself. And that felt to me like the primary block to finding love. The me I imagined I could be would be loved. It was just the me I was that fell short. And love was just one of the goals; there were others, achievements that would flow from being better, being different. It did not occur to me—or to any of us—that we could never do all we wanted not because of the limitations of talent, but because of the limitations of life. We did not yet know that each choice involves a loss, that love demands sacrifice, that achievement exacts a price.

I ask young couples who come to me to be married what they envision as the obstacles to their future. Some mention money, some talk about the other's family, a few perhaps speak about some trait in the other or in themselves that must be dealt with and overcome. What they rarely realize is that the world will ask things of them that are different from what they will ask of each other, and that each concession to the world threatens to breed resentment. Sometimes work will come to seem happier than home. Friends will appear more sympathetic than one's spouse. Renewing love will be an act of will and of faith.

There is a story by Somerset Maugham called "The Colonel's Lady." It is about a bluff English gentleman and his wife. He is a stereotype, a man who buries his nose behind the morning paper, hunts, goes to the club, and despite living with his wife has not truly *seen* her in years. They are childless—instead of having descendants, he lives in a world of walls covered with the paintings of his ancestors. His wife is quiet, and she seems sweet and shy.

One day a book is delivered to the house. It turns out that it is a book of poems written by the colonel's wife. The colonel reacts with amused indulgence: "Well, you know, poetry isn't much in my line, but —yes, I'd like a copy." He thinks the whole thing rather nice, if strange, and gives her a patronizing smile before turning back to his paper. He is not curious; he tries to read the book, but it makes little sense to him.

Soon, however, all of London is talking about the poems. They are erotic, vivid. In striking images, the poems describe a torrid affair. The colonel grudgingly attends a party of literary people to celebrate his wife's success, and he hears someone remark that such a book must have come out of real experience because it is too vibrant to be wholly imaginative.

Now the colonel is in a tizzy. He does not know what to do, and he seeks the advice of others. His friends tell him to forget about it. There is no point in dragging up what could only be painful. At first, he is inclined to take this advice. "It's no use crying over spilt milk," he says. Then, illustrating both his smugness and the gulf that has arisen between them, he muses, "But there's one thing I'll never understand to my dying day—what in the name of heaven did the fellow ever see in her?"

In time, however, the internal pressure builds, and the colonel cannot help himself. There is puzzlement and hurt in his eyes as he looks at the wife whom he thought he knew. He confronts her and asks if the poems are based on truth. She begs him to forget it, but he will not. Finally she confesses, yes, they are based on reality. Do I know the man? he thunders. In a meek voice, she admits that he does, and begs him not to go any further. But he cannot stop now, and demands to know who it is.

Finally, in a soft voice, his wife answers, "It was you. It was you—as you were—all those years ago—in those happy days when we first met, and you loved me." Her husband responds incredulously that the poems say that the lover died. He did, replies his wife. "The man that loved me died."

Over the years they have lost each other. In that loss he has also lost part of himself.

Sometimes it is the addition of love that we create in our lives that sharpens the pang of its absence. When Friday night falls, the minimum candles lit for Sabbath are two. In many homes it is customary when children are born to add a candle for each child. When the children leave, the number of candles is not diminished. According to the law, one may increase light but not diminish it. The blaze lingers even in the absence of the one for whom the candle was originally added. The words of Indonesian writer Pramoedya Ananta Toer give us an image of creating room in one's life. In an interview a few years ago in *The New Yorker,* Toer said of his home, "This is a big house with many empty rooms, because I added a room for each of the children as they were born. Now they have all left."

We create space for love, and when love leaves, the space remains.

The metaphor of love as a filling of hollow spaces sometimes feels like more than a metaphor. We know that feeling of hollowness inside when someone we love is with someone else. The hollowness, and the feeling of fullness when we are with someone we love, is a physical sensation, more than a metaphor. Each person, with age, builds or closes down rooms in the soul. Some people's capacity for love grows; others' shrinks. How do we react to the loss of love?

There are a number of miracle stories of mystics who walked heedless of their footing and stepped right off cliffs. God simply extended their footing so that they never knew they had imperiled themselves. Similarly, the beloved provides the foundation so that one's stride is supported. Accomplishment is spurred by knowing that one is loved. Daring is urged by the knowledge that one's footing is solid, that behind or beneath one's efforts is a foundation of love. Take away the foundation, and the fall is inevitable. Love and faith provide footing in remarkably similar ways. They both fill us, and one leads to the other.

To be truly filled with faith is to know the possibilities of love.

King David is at once a lover of God, of women, and of power. In these intersecting and often clashing passions, David has a complex life with his children.

The first child born of his adulterous liaison with Bathsheba dies. While the child remained alive, David wept and prayed. At the infant's death, he arises, dusts himself off, and prepares to meet the world. David bluntly explains his behavior to his attendants: "While the child was still alive, I fasted and wept because I thought: 'Who knows? The Lord may have pity on me, and the child may live.' But now that he is dead, why should I fast? Can I bring him back again? I shall go to him, but he will never come back to me" (II Sam. 12:22–23).

Yet David behaves quite differently with his son Absalom. Absalom rebels against him and leads an armed force in an attempt to overthrow his father. This action may seem unthinkable to us, but throughout history, kings have had most to fear from their own families, particularly their children. The more brutal monarchs, like Herod, simply slaughtered their kin. Some of the wiser kings avoided this rivalry. As Louis XIV said, "If

I must fight, it shall be with my enemies rather than with my children."

David suppresses the rebellion but tries to ensure that Absalom will be spared. The commander of his troops, Joab, realizes that this sentimental plea is dangerous for David's reign, and oversees Absalom's execution. When David hears of Absalom's death, his reaction is quite different from the one he had to the loss of his previous child: "The king was shaken. He went up to the upper chamber of the gateway and wept, moaning these words as he went, 'My son Absalom! O my son, my son Absalom! If only I had died instead of you! O Absalom, my son, my son!' " (II Sam. 18:33)

Why is David's attitude so different? After the death of his child with Bathsheba, he is almost nonchalant. After Absalom's, he is devastated. Perhaps because Absalom is older, and David has known him as a person. Perhaps because they have been estranged, and David feels he might have acted differently— although the other child was condemned by David's sin, it was born of the same sin.

Another possibility exists. The death of Absalom is the confirmation of the conflict David has always known. He cannot successfully balance his loves. They must entail loss. This hard truth is pointed out to him by Joab. Joab tells David that his mourning for Absalom, his son who rebelled, might estrange the troops who fought for David to overcome Absalom. He can cry for his son, or ensure the continuity of his kingdom. He cannot do both.

I thought of this story when a couple came to see me about the future of their business. The husband had spent his entire working life creating a business that was now extensive and complex. He loved the business and did not want to see it die with him. Together, he and his wife had one son.

The wife wanted desperately for the business to be left to the son. The husband refused. He loved his son, he told me. He loved him deeply. But he would destroy the business, and in the end that would benefit no one. His wife argued that given the chance, he would flourish; it was because he had always been overwhelmed by his father that he had not shown his true quality. The father felt himself torn between competing loves and competing responsibilities. If his son was unworthy, he told me, then he would be condemning the hundreds of people who work for him to lose their jobs. "But," pleaded his wife, "this is your son."

The decision was made for them. The son, tired of being pulled and doubted, told his father that he would under no circumstances accept the business. He was out, and the father could leave it to whomever he wanted. But everyone who knows the son feels that he carries the wound of being distrusted deep within him. The business, presumably, will be saved. The family is in tatters.

Loss can be blunted and entombed, like it was for Dickens's Miss Havisham, sitting alone in her tattered bridal dress with the moldering wedding cake; fresh losses are nothing to her because she has made her life a shrine to an old loss. Alternately, one can simply be destroyed by loss, crushed into immobility by its weight. For David, who keeps himself alive, loss is an ever threatening possibility. Each step of life is dangerous, because he loves. The life potion that ensures pain is desire. David continues to have faith, to hope in the world, and to want things from the world. Therefore, he will continue to lose.

For years in the local club in which I played chess, there was a young prodigy who was universally thought to be very promising. Once he played in a prestigious tournament and was tied for the lead. In the final game, the prize was almost his. He had a tremendous advantage, and it should have been a mere matter of routine to convert it into a win. But instead he made a terrible blunder. With it, he lost the game and the tournament.

More significant, with it he lost the concentration that enabled him to play chess. The loss was so devastating to him that he could not recover. He would play that single game over and over in his head. He could not escape the sense that with that one mistake, he had thrown everything away. All his other games became insignificant. Even though he made but one mistake, he lost his belief in himself. Through this one loss, he suffered a permanent failure of faith.

This is the hub of the relation between love and loss. The more keenly we desire something—a person, a state of being, a piece of our own history—the more savage is its loss. Proust's renowned novel, traditionally translated *Remembrance of Things Past*, is more accurately translated *In Search of Lost Time*. Proust's ultimately quixotic task is to recapture what has been lost, and the fundamental loss is time. However eloquently he may recapture his memories on the page, what he remembers is gone. What embroiders his novel with the piercing beauty of great art is not merely that the places and people he evokes are gone, however, but that they are gone—and they were loved.

Not the past alone, but the loved past causes us pain. The

older couple peering across the breakfast table at each other see
in the lines and marks of age the simulacrum of shared years.
Like travelers, they look back on the distance they have tra-
versed and marvel not only at its vastness but at the way all the
distress of the journey melds with its sweetness and seems dear.
The pain—that which was endurable and could be overcome—
becomes part of the loved journey. And in the word "loved" is
the intimation of loss.

There is no deep love without loss. The losses of life chip
away, in infinite combinations, at the attachments of human
beings. The test of love is the flexibility and fidelity with which
partners can forgive, recall, and manage the vicissitudes of love,
and of betrayal. For the strange mixture of love and betrayal
exists not only in those whom we choose to love; it exists also
within our birth families, which are antecedent to choice.

In lectures about the dynamics of family, I used to tell groups
that God gave us families to teach us to love people with whom
we might otherwise not even be friends. Families are complicated. The astute reader of literature realizes that most of the
intrigues, the deceptions, the conflicts occur within families. For
families are composed of human beings, and we are volatile
creatures.

But inside families, this volatility is complicated by history,
closeness, and love. The losses inside families are different.
From the very first days of birth, a child becomes part of the
rites of love and loss.

Out of 100 counseling situations that arise in the course of
the average year, more than 70 percent involve family. Parents
fret over wayward children. Children complain about befuddled

or misguided parents. Couples stumble over each other's sensitivities. Cruelties that streak the human personality tend to come out most vividly at home.

In preparing couples for marriage, I try to clarify for them that the creation of the new family must to some degree entail the loss of the old. Not everyone is prepared for the loss. One wedding was canceled a week before the ceremony. The bride-to-be had at last realized that in the groom's mind, his mother came first. When the bride and her prospective mother-in-law clashed, the groom invariably supported his mother. She had been widowed, and that fact was the sun around which everything had to orbit. While telling his fiancée that she was first in his life, he also believed that it was her task to integrate herself into the already complex enmeshments of his family. She loved him, and he did love her. But he could not face losing the earlier attachment.

When the engagement dissolved, his family—his brothers, his mother—told him what a good decision he had made and how she was not right for him. But the decision was hers, and the truth was that the marriage was not right for the brothers and the mother.

Once more the issue is faith, and faith's offspring: courage. Leaving the old, creating the new requires faith. I have always found it significant that the Torah ends—at the close of the book of Deuteronomy—with the death of Moses. Immediately after reading that section, we turn back to the beginning of the scroll and read about the creation of the world. Death precedes creation. Loss gives way to renewal. But only if one believes this cycle can one risk losing, or bear to lose. If everything is static, then each loss is irrevocable. In a faithless world, loss is only sadness.

In the biblical creation story, God ultimately pronounces the world "good." This world is to be embraced, ingested, greedily explored for the wonders God has given. The variety and depth of the offerings given to us in this world are designed to expand and deepen our souls. We must rope ourselves to the world's wonders and feel its losses. For ultimately our end in this world is to grow in soul. The soul grows through pain as well as joy. Out of pain comes the steepest growth because the resources of the soul are most severely taxed. We grow spiritual muscle by understanding that avoiding pain is sidestepping growth. Also, when we avoid pain we narrow our lives. In the end we are not spared, because increasingly things in the world are seen as occasions for suffering instead of opportunities to grow.

The Bible conveys its truth bluntly. We are told that after the last Egyptian plague, "there was no house where there was not someone dead" (Ex. 12:30). That is exactly the truth. In each house in life, there is loss. In each person's story, there is pain; there is love forced to accept rejection and negation.

We cannot love as adults until we understand that love is never free from pain. The losses of love are what propel us through our selfishness, through the shells of our selves, to the other. And through each genuine encounter with another, there is a glimpse of something still greater, eternity that peeks through the other's eyes.

The Sassover Rebbe said that he learned the meaning of love from overhearing a conversation between two villagers. One asked the other, "Do you love me?" The second replied, "I love you deeply." The first asked, "Do you know, my friend, what gives me pain?" The second protested that he could not possibly know. "If you do not know what gives me pain," lamented the first, "how can you say you love me?"

The roots of love are bound up with a knowledge of pain and a consciousness of loss. In the end, such love connects us to God. A sense of ultimacy returns us with renewed fire to our beloveds. The aura of eternity envelops a love that is encircled in a passion of faith; eroticism is tinged with deeper dimensions of meaning. The human body is not only an end but a conduit for two people to express a fidelity beyond each other. Their joining is an act not only of love but of affirmation and of faith.

Six

Faith

May God deny you peace but give you glory.
—*Miguel De Unamuno*, The Tragic Sense of Life

After fleeing Egypt, Israel camped at the foot of the mount of Sinai. The wanderers had been slaves. They were a frightened people. They clung to their leader, Moses, and to the hope of an invisible God.

When Moses disappeared up the mountain, the people's courage failed. Though they had experienced the miraculous escape from Egypt, now they were scared. They watched, and saw nothing but the sweeping, shifting sands. They waited, and heard only silence. This dazed people stood, waiting for something, some sign that the world was not empty. The wilderness gave them nothing. They huddled together in fear, remembering the chariots of Pharaoh, the years of bondage. Surely they wanted to have faith, but their faith was conquered by fear.

They built the calf, they danced and sang around it, and their spirits revived. The calf gave them a chance to fill the stillness with song. However forced the reverie, it felt better to them than the barrenness of the desert.

For those who did not join the celebration, was it because they could tolerate the emptiness of silence, or because they did not feel empty?

During my teenage years, I was an ardent, thoroughgoing atheist. I was twelve years old when I saw the movie *Night and Fog*, a documentary about the Holocaust. On the screen were horrors beyond what I had ever seen or imagined. I saw bull-dozers piling bodies into large pits. I saw a world bereft of God.

I did not leave the movie angry. Perhaps I should have, but, instead, I felt empty inside. People had done these things, and people had not stopped it. *We* made the difference in the world, yet we all were alone. God was irrelevant. We did not admit it, but the earth spun in a void. The horror bespoke the truth about things. I felt sick deep, deep within, a sickness that has never entirely gone away.

It was not just that there was suffering and evil in God's world. It was the scale, the constant unrelenting pain, the tragedies small and large that litter the landscape of every life. My intel-lectual hero became the English philosopher Bertrand Russell, whose keen and quick arguments against religion supported my own instincts. Russell spoke eloquently of religion's cruelties, the ways it sacrificed people to doctrine.

Most corrosive was Russell's mockery. He made fun of reli-gious people's foibles, like their distrust of science. "People used to say that faith moved mountains, and no one believed it," wrote Russell. "Now we say the atom bomb moves mountains, and everyone believes it."

Russell pressed particularly hard on the question of evil. How can a good God permit the brutality of the world to continue? Moreover, in parts of sacred scripture, God not only permits cruelty but commands it. Perhaps it is safer, Russell wrote, to assume that a demon created the world when God was not looking.

The logic of Russell's writing, its cool wit, captured me. Religion was a crutch, unworthy of free people. If we were smarter, stronger, we would realize that the God we worship was modeled on "Oriental despotisms" and was no better than the people who thought Him up. In its quarrel with science, religion repeatedly, grudgingly, gave way, because science was truth.

Part of my conviction that God didn't exist was based on my feeling that those who believed were somehow weaker than I was. They needed a God to support the world because they could not face what I saw as the lonely, cold cosmos, a place utterly disinterested in our day-to-day living and dying. To me, those who believed in God were unwilling to shoulder the sky. I imagined myself courageous enough to face the dark without anyone or anything to prop me up. I had all the mighty conviction of a teenager.

The older I got, the more life challenged my preconception about strength of character. In the face of difficulties, I saw religious people draw dignity from a source I couldn't fathom. I saw that everyone is afflicted with suffering and weakness, the atheist no less than the believer. No one is perfectly logical in their dealings with others. Passions bend all of us. A thousand obscure forces, from breeding to genes to the mysteries of character, act on everyone. People of faith are not the only ones with crutches—we all hobble.

More important, I discovered that Russell's underlying premise was a mistake. Weakness is not always a distortion. Sometimes a weakness allows one to see more of the truth than does strength.

In my own relationships, I realized that when I was weaker, I was truer. When I was growing up, the correct response to "How are you?" was "Fine." Nothing was ever wrong. Weaknesses, tears, problems, helplessness were not exactly shameful, but certainly not matters of pride. In time, I discovered that there was a joy, a freedom in telling the truth about my stumblings. Less hidden, I was more accessible, both to myself and to others. The "perfect" cannot be touched by other people or by God; there is no place to enter if the heart feels itself whole.

The ancient Greek lesson of the wound and the bow shows that debility is the cousin of creativity. Learning it was, for me, a long time in coming. But as a teenager, I did not believe in the vitality of weakness. Strength was the banner I chose to carry through the world.

As I got older, I asked myself what it was inside of me that had created this certainty of an empty cosmos. To my surprise, I discovered that my love of "strength" was a mask for my fear. It grew out of the relative coziness of childhood and into the wildness of being a teenager. Toys and bedtime tales gave way to puberty, sexual yearnings, and general confusion. To be perfectly rational was a way out of the things happening to me that I did not understand. Like many teenagers, I was drawn to people who seemed to have it all figured out, who did not have turbulence in their souls. I read Sherlock Holmes, I watched the rational Mr. Spock, and I listened to Bertrand Russell.

As I began to understand how vicious the world could be, I found it hard to believe that a God could preside over such a mess. Was God indifferent, or powerless?

To believe is to risk being duped. The fear of being made a fool kept me far from faith. It was easier for me to have an image of being a tough-minded, steel-spined atheist who is willing to see the world as it is than a muddled, frightened, and hopeful believer. I did not want to be fooled, to find myself gullible. I treasured Russell's answer to a reporter who asked him what he would say if one day, after death, he found himself before God. "I should ask Him why he did not provide more evidence," answered Russell. It was not our fault. We were simply being rational.

Neither reason nor emotion was adequate for coping with the central question of life. I have never been able to think about God without thinking about evil. Atheism offered no respite, and belief no sanctuary. Since the day I saw *Night and Fog*, the question will not leave me alone.

This past year, one of my congregants, Rose Farkas, published a book called *Ruchele*, about her memories of life before World War II, during the war, and after. She endured the concentration camps, and after her liberation, she found a world shattered. In a book filled with painful reminiscences, she writes as follows.

Finally I found it—a white oval sign with a fat red cross in the middle and around the cross in red letters the words The International Swiss Red Cross Orphanage. I rang the doorbell. No answer. I knocked on the door to the entrance hall—no answer. I pushed on the door handle—it was open. Inside two staircases led to the upper floors. A strange muffled moan came from upstairs. Following it I found the children in a large smelly, dark room huddled together trying to warm themselves with their own bodies. They were shivering and crying softly. The same scene was repeated in the next room. I saw a little girl holding the hand of a small boy who was lying on the floor. When I approached, I could see that the boy was dead. I told the little girl to let go of him. "I can't," she said crying. "My mommy told me never to let go of his hand."

So where was God? It doesn't matter how many stories you hear. Each new tragedy renews the question: Where is God?

What I learned at twelve was not that faith is impossible but that it will never be easy. At first it seemed impossible. Whatever faith I have today does not represent a return to the certainties of childhood. It is wrested from a world that I saw very clearly at twelve years old. I was not wrong about the inhumanity that swirls about us. My heart is still sick. I am no less perplexed or pained. The loss of faith at that moment almost thirty years ago was in its way final. What I did not know was that real faith can be built on loss.

Living with reason alone will keep one safe in this world, far away from the twisting of the heart. But being safe is the opposite of being saved. To be saved—which means not supernatural redemption but the ability to love and be loved, to be broken and become whole again—we need more than our minds. We need the faith that springs from the soul.

What fosters or hinders faith? Why is it that one person's suffering deepens his faith, and another's suffering destroys his faith? Hidden amid the mysteries we cannot account for is a confusion about faith.

Faith is most often heard today in the phrase "faith in oneself." That is not faith. Faith is the certainty in something greater than oneself. To believe in one's own powers is self-confidence. Faith in oneself has too small a circumference.

Faith is the belief that what we see is not all. Faith is not knowledge of what the mystery of the universe is, but the conviction that there is a mystery, that it is greater than us, that it is not subject to human understanding.

What I did not understand about Russell's writings when I was younger is that behind them is the same fear that I read them to escape. I began to read about Russell's life and discovered that this supremely rational man lived through a series of broken, bitter relationships. His life was the opposite of the calm, detached order of his writing. As a guide to life, then, his words had little reason to be trusted.

But, more important, I came to see his confidence as arrogance. The religious people I knew whom I respected had a rootedness that by comparison made Russell seem flimsy. Their relationship to something beyond themselves made his humor sound shrill. He was no less dogmatic than the believers he criticized. But beyond both there was a different kind of believer; this kind did not have to convince—he had only to live. The deep believer's faith was enacted, not argued. That such people existed was better evidence for there being a God than any argument.

Faith, as I came to understand it, is a recognition that there is something ultimately mysterious and deeply beautiful about the world. We cannot fully understand it or plot it out. Some may be uncomfortable with the term "God," but whatever you call the mystery, it does not stand aloof. We can enter into it, come closer to it, in some way join it.

Still I could not, and cannot, give up my reason in order to have faith. Earlier doubts do not disappear, at least mine have not. I cannot surrender the voice in my head that expresses reservations and objections. Even more, I cannot suppress my heartsickness in order to have faith. The sound of suffering that calls God into question each day will not go away. I wish for a faith that requires an open heart but does not require the abandonment of my head. I search for a faith that allows the two to work in concert, so that reason and logic become not the enemy of faith but its partner.

For me, the path toward having faith is the path not of scientific reflection but of using my mind to see how faith can unfold ever deeper layers of myself and of human life. Study enables me to reach into deeper parts of myself, to reach out of deeper parts of myself. When I engage with someone else through the printed page, someone who lived at another time but struggled with the same issues, I find that the shared human struggle inspires me and comforts me. But I no longer enjoy what I once relished, the intellectual argument about whether God exists. For me it is a game I have no patience to play. I used to love the argument. Now it seems foolish.

In my life, the aim of the game was miscast from the beginning. I could not come to faith by finding the right argument. Instead, I uneasily inhabit faith each day by renewing my struggle to experience it, to know myself, and to appreciate all we have been given. For me, doing so means constantly reminding myself that I usually experience the world on one level, inattentively, even thoughtlessly. But pausing to see deeper connections, to feel gratitude for what I have, to feel the fleetingness of these many gifts, reorients me. Suddenly I am not simply eating an apple, I am tasting it, being grateful for it, acknowledging the everyday miraculousness of it. Exceptional moments in life are precious, but the ordinary sacredness is what we all have the potential to share. Looking into myself, examining my actions and thoughts, becoming aware of my movement through the world and through the lives of those whom I touch—such focus does not erase all doubts, but it does intensify the experience of living. More, it helps to remind me, by tying me to so many others who seek the same vividness in life and reality beyond, that I am not alone.

I spent two years as a director of a library. We used to get calls all the time from people who wanted to give away their books. Often we declined, since the world is so glutted with books and most of the time what was offered were copies of books we already had in our collection. But one day I received a call from an old woman whose voice was so urgent that I could not say no.

I went to her home. She had been calling for weeks, insisting that she had books of great value and beauty. I entered an old and dirty apartment. It was filled with bits of flea-market finery, small silver baubles, and colored glass bottles on footstools and windowsills. She ushered me in and showed me, with pride, her

books. There were some paperback novels, and a set of ten or
eleven Horizon books, containing articles on art, literature, and
other cultural subjects. These were her treasures, and she made
a show of reluctance in parting with them.

As I offered the appropriate exclamations of appreciation, she
answered the unspoken question: "I am giving them to you
because I do not have family to give them to. I am afraid that I
will die and someone will just take them. Maybe my neighbor
will come in and get them. I don't want just anyone to have
them." I nodded. I understood. I took them.

For this woman, to give her books to a library was to create
a link with immortality. We lose so many things in life—friends,
family, jobs—that fear of loss becomes an organizing principle
of our lives. For her the question was, What could survive? If
the books went to a library, then she was not entirely lost.
Something of herself, her contribution, would endure. Giving
those books was an act of faith against fear.

Deep inside the fear of loss is the fear of aloneness.
"Friendship or death," says the Talmud, with startling intensity.
Being alone is the first fear. The heart of faith is believing one
is never alone.

Our faith has been whittled away in battle with all the disciplines that answer the riddles of the world: natural science,
social science, technology, the humanities. Faith that asks
religion to explain the phenomenon of the natural world is
faith doomed to irrelevance. Faith charts the course of a life.
It does not map out the stars or tell us the age of the universe.

Faith orients us in the cosmos, but it does not predict the weather.

When we lose God, we do not lose the yearning for God. Inside us is the constant thumping hope that all this means something, that our lives are somehow lasting, that our years and loves are not hollow. "From out of the depth I call unto you, O God" (Psalms 130:1). The cry from the depths reaches higher than the cry from the heights. But it is also the more frightening one, for to be disappointed when we are low is that much more devastating. Everywhere we look, the same lesson is being taught. To reach toward God from loss of faith is most powerful.

This reaching is not an intellectual process. The Hebrew word for faith, *bitachon*, really means trust. Trust is not always a process of thought. It is real, immediate, enveloping.

Yearning for God is the hunger that most often goes unrecognized in our lives. Other hungers are satisfied, sometimes on an epic scale, but they are not enough. The cliché of a man indulging himself, making tremendous amounts of money and still being unhappy, has its source in this simple truth. Having an insatiable appetite for sensual pleasure, for food, for money is a consequence of trying to satisfy the hidden hunger for something greater than what we can know. It is as if we have two reservoirs inside, one for sensual appetites and one for the spirit, and by filling the first we hope to fill the second. But the only things that can satisfy spiritual cravings are things of the spirit.

Elie Wiesel told the following tale of a young man, assailed by doubts, who seeks the solace of a rebbe.

When a Jew can provide no answer, he at least has a tale to tell. And so Rabbi Pinhas of Koretz invited the visitor to come closer, and then he said with a smile: "Know, my young friend, that what is happening to you also happened to me. When I was your age I stumbled over the same obstacles. I, too, was filled with questionings and doubts. About man and his fate, creation and its meaning. I was struggling with so many dark forces that I could not advance; I was wallowing in doubt, locked in despair. I tried study, prayer, meditation. In vain. Penitence, silence, solitude. In vain. My doubts remained doubts, my questions remained threats. Impossible to proceed, to project myself into the future. I simply could not go on. Then one day I learned that the Rebbe Israel Baal Shem Tov would be coming to our town. Curiosity led me to the shtibel where he was receiving his followers. When I entered he was finishing the Amidah prayer. He turned around and saw me, and I was convinced that he was seeing me, me and no one else—but so was everyone else in the room. His gaze overwhelmed me, and I felt less alone. And strangely, I was able to go home, open the Talmud, and plunge into my studies once more. You see," said Rebbe Pinhas of Koretz, "the questions remained questions. But I was able to go on."

Faith is in part about the simple certainty that we are not alone. The young person in Wiesel's story above has discovered that the world is a more knotty, recalcitrant, and unkind place than he imagined. Doubts are more prevalent than dreams. But there are also more kindnesses than he knew.

Jean-Paul Sartre wrote of waiting for someone at a café. Everyone who comes is noticed for *not* being the person he is waiting for. All of his energies, thoughts, emotions are focused on the one who is absent. So does he think about God, wrote Sartre. His being is attuned to the absence. Beckett's *Waiting for Godot* is the theatrical embodiment of this phenomenon. Godot never arrives, and the audience is keenly focused on the character who is not there. The one who is absent is, by that very absence, most powerfully present.

In the Bible, the great parable of questioning faith is the story of Job, but Job never really loses faith that God exists. God is all too real to Job. Job questions not God's power, but God's justice.

At the beginning of the book, Job is the wealthiest man in the East. He is abundantly blessed. Job has a wonderful family and great riches. He is as pious as he is fortunate. Job carefully tends to his relationship with God, offering sacrifices at every opportunity.

As the drama begins, the adversarial angel insists that Job loves God because God has given him so much. What child would not profess love for so generous a parent? "But take away all he has," God is told, "and he will curse you to your face" (1:11).

Devastating losses soon follow. Job is stripped of everything. While he never quite curses God—his first words, indeed, are to bless God—he does launch a lengthy diatribe. His anger at the injustice of God knows no bounds. His faith has been stunned by the force of the blow. That blow has jarred loose anger and grievance.

But perhaps Job's response proves the adversarial angel's point. Job did not love God—Job loved the goods that God dispensed. Job loved his life. Job loved his stature, his wealth, his family. To love God would have meant continuing to love God in the face of catastrophe.

The beginning of the book posits a perfectly righteous man.

Yet in a test of his goodness, God permits Job to be cruelly afflicted. Job does not respond by wondering whether God exists—he never doubts that God is the author of the anguish visited upon him. What Job wonders is whether the God who exists is a cruel or a kind God. After Job has suffered unjustly, God emerges from the whirlwind to ask a series of utterly irrelevant questions. He asks if Job was around when the world was created. He asks if Job can perform great feats of strength. God seems to flex His celestial muscles. But Job has never insisted that he, Job, created the world—only that God did so incorrectly, unfairly.

Why does God lecture about the creation of the world? Perhaps it is to inform Job that the world was not created the way he believes it was. God ultimately tells Job that faith cannot meet the test of success, that God's world cannot conform to our standards. There is no inherent goodness meted out in this world to those who are good. Punishment is not always stored up for those who do evil. The idea that this is a fair world—and that therefore Job is entitled to redress—is Job's idea, not God's. God has made a world filled with beauty, splendor, strength, majesty, awe. The task of making it moral falls on us.

I have read the story of Job many times, and studied many of the interpretations of the book. For me, Job comes down to a stark choice. He cannot continue to believe in a God who makes the world fair. The world is not fair, and the book does not let us believe for a moment that if we only knew more we would realize that everything really is fair. Injustice exists. So long as Job is concerned only for justice, for fairness, he cannot come close to God, because the indictment will never end. The world will never work the way Job is certain it should. And Job has substituted justice for God—an important but smaller concept for the grandest idea of all.

Faith should have a different basis. Maybe fairness is Job's responsibility, to the extent he can carry it out in this world. Maybe the demands Job makes on God, that God be this way or do that, are what block his faith. Thinking we know what God should be creates a sort of block to experiencing what God is in our lives. There is a strange Rabbinic statement that one should bless God for bad things as one does for good things. Believing that God must guard us from losing—and if we lose, God does not care or does not exist—will keep us outside of faith.

When Job does overcome his distance, his compensation is great. He discovers a God who will not arrange the world to his liking, but who will address him. Job takes the encounter as a substitute for an ideal balance of the scales of justice. Job draws closer to God at the end of the book, a God who has caused him so much suffering. Yet hovering in the background is a sturdier doubt: Perhaps Job is compensated, but what of us?

Job speaks to us because we too have lost faith. Perhaps it was momentary, perhaps we lost only fragments of our faith. Sometimes loss can be a clearing of the debris that separates us from God. We think we know what it is God should be doing, if there is a God, but when we suffer some loss, we no longer can hold that conception of God. We are forced to explore anew. The great physicist Richard Feynmann once remarked half-jokingly that the great discoveries in physics are made by young scientists because they have not yet learned too much to destroy their ability to be creative. Once we know, as Job learned, that God will not always clear our path in this world, we may be ready for a relationship based less on need and more on love.

What of the losses that drive us further from faith? The Talmud tells of one rabbi named Elisha ben Abuyah. He is known as Acher, "the other." He was a rabbi who, in the vivid Talmudic imagery, "cut the roots." He was the only Talmudic teacher who became an atheist and abandoned his Judaism.

The bare facts of the story, filtered through the distortions of time, seem to be these: Elisha ben Abuyah was one of the leading young lights of his day (his day was the early second century of the common era, some 1,900 years ago). He studied with his fellow rabbis, including Rabbi Akiva, commonly acknowledged as the greatest of the Talmudic Rabbis. His teacher was the gentle and profound scholar Rabbi Joshua. Not only did ben Abuyah possess a brilliant legal mind, but he was involved in some sort of mystical practice with Rabbi Akiva and others. What exactly those practices were is not certain, and we do not know for sure how they might have affected his fate.

Yet some experience, or combination of experiences, drove him away from the Jewish tradition. One account says that while witnessing the deaths and degradation of other scholars, he found himself unable to believe in a God who presides over such injustice.

Another account relates to the biblical commandment of chasing the mother bird away when taking eggs from her nest (Deut. 22:6–7). The commandment is a humane injunction to ensure that the mother will not witness her children being taken, and to protect her, so that the entire family will not be destroyed at once. The Bible continues by assuring that if you observe this commandment, "you may fare well and have a long life." Elisha ben Abuyah once saw a man who climbed a palm tree on the Sabbath and took a mother bird and her eggs from a nest. Despite having violated both the prohibition from Deuteronomy and the Sabbath laws, the man climbed down unharmed. After the Sabbath, another man climbed a tree and shooed away a mother bird, yet upon reaching the ground was bitten by a snake and died. Careful observance of God's law seemed to have no relation to one's ultimate fate. Quoting the Bible, ben Abuyah said: "It is written: 'Let the mother go, and take only the young, in order that you may fare well and have a long life.' Where is the goodness and long life for this man?"

"There is no justice, and there is no Judge" sums up Elisha ben Abuyah's instant, horrified conclusion. The center of the universe dropped out from beneath him in one moment. There are indications that he began to pursue Greek wisdom, substituting the secular speculations of philosophy for religious teachings.

Like every member of the clergy, I have delivered eulogies where I must stand up and ask the same question. Good people, parents with young children, young men and women not yet married, have lived exemplary lives and died long before their promises were fulfilled. Is there justice, and is there a Judge? If we don't ask the question, we betray the memory of the one who died. Can I say to the grieving family, or even to myself, that we must bless God for the bad as well as the good? Each time there is a suitable answer, each time it seems one can rest, as if by design life strikes with a new tragedy.

Elisha ben Abuyah was tortured by the contradictions built

into a religious worldview. How can the act of serving God bring about calamity? Even if God fails to punish wickedness, how could God penalize goodness? The unfairness drove the faith from him, leaving him hollow.

Losses reverberate through the centuries. Elisha ben Abuyah's loss of faith, two thousand years later, inspired a novel by the American rabbi Milton Steinberg, titled *As a Driven Leaf*. Taking the scattered Talmudic texts that refer to Elisha ben Abuyah, Steinberg constructed a world and a scenario. In his eyes, the lapsed rabbi was always attracted to the glitter of the secular world. Doubts plagued him throughout his life. He was, in Steinberg's reckoning, a very modern man.

Steinberg follows his tale through the academies of the Rabbis and the Roman court. The two worlds are placed side by side, each with its merit, and each with its limitations. Rome boasts a beauty, a sophistication, and even a savagery that glitters and seduces. Its learning is real and, at times, its laws just. In the Rabbinical world of the time, there is a deep piety and insularity that is noble but stifling. The two worlds war within the breast of Elisha ben Abuyah.

Elisha ben Abuyah was someone who yearned for the consolations of faith, but he could not still the voice that told him that certainty is a chimera, that the world has no guide, that justice is a human invention. His dilemma is our own. The forces we believe in are impersonal forces: not goodness but gravity. We do not doubt the laws of thermodynamics, but the worth of our lives is a daily, agonizing issue. We are captured by the sophisticated wonder of all the marvels modern society has created. Is there a place inside this world for faith?

The difference between Job and Elisha is that Elisha became

deadened, while Job became outraged—a crucial difference
when the losses of life strike. Outrage is a reaction to life. The
heat of anger is far sounder, psychologically and even theologically, than a resignation to despair. Despair severs a relationship. Anger challenges it. Fury is frightening, but indifference is
deadening.

Anger at God is anger at the absence of God's healing power
in this world. For all the candles lit, the prayers poured forth,
the devotion upraised to the heavens, human pain is undimin-
ished. The lesson of Job seems to take on clearer outlines. We
are not meant to have a God to part seas and heal broken limbs.
God must be a God of relationship. The highest human relationships are not based on what we can get from one another.
True love has an element of disinterest—it loves the other without thought of what it can get in return. True love has an element of abandon, past calculation. Perhaps the book of Job
ultimately teaches this lesson. At the beginning of the book,
Job's love for God is contingent—if God will provide, Job will
remain attached. When God no longer provides, Job gives way
to rage.

The root of many problems of faith is a misunderstanding
encouraged by religion itself. We are often told that if only we
are good, or act a certain way, God will reward us. Then we are
struck by the losses of life. We see that there is no power that
will save us from loss. Our means of navigating through difficult
times, the certainty of meaning, is snatched from us. If the universe has no guidance, whether we call it God or not, then how
can our loss have any meaning?

Establishing ourselves in the universe on the basis of quid pro
quo cannot be right, however. There must be a better basis

for relationship than this simple exchange of goods that some imagine is what being close to God is truly about. Meaning must be based on something deeper than my hope to be helped to success. Love is focused on the other, and on the transformation of the beloved to become worthier.

In times of crisis in my life, I pray, and I am caught in a contradiction. For I believe that I am praying for the strength to endure whatever will happen. Yet I cannot help hoping that God will somehow save the situation. I do not believe in a God who takes out tumors, yet I cannot help praying for such a result. I visit people in the hospital each week, and I wonder if it is possible to care about a God who can help but will not. Still I return to the same thought: If God matters only because God does things for us, then God does not really matter at all; only we matter. Is God important only insofar as God dispenses favors? Can we reach high enough in our hearts to love God, to be open to faith, no matter what has happened to us in this world? Can we use loss as a platform to believe that although God does not prevent loss, God is there to help us create meaning from what has happened?

While we cannot count on miracles to save us, we can be miraculous. We can ourselves do things that change the world and reshape our own souls. Faith teaches us not that life will be easy, but that the difficulties of life yield beauty.

There is a story of a man who looked up at the heavens and said, "Dear God, there is so much pain and anguish in your world—why don't you send help?" And God answered, "I did send help—I sent you."

From misfortune, meaning; from sadness, significance.

———

One gauge of the intensity of faith is the intensity of grieving for its loss. True loss of faith is debilitating. The world shudders. Meaning is drained away.

A young woman who was anhedonic once came to see me. She took no pleasure in anything. Before making an appointment, she wrote me a long letter describing her predicament. "I feel completely lost in the world. I have no direction in life and feel as if I am only taking up space." She had suffered many hurts. The God who she once believed would protect her seemed to have abandoned her.

That was the most powerful blow. The certainty of being helped was shattered, and with it went her confidence in the world. Gradually her circle got narrower and narrower, until it seemed she was in a straitjacket.

After some time talking with her, I understood what had become of her faith. It was a faith that was essentially centered in her own fate. She needed to enlarge her faith to include others. I encouraged her to work in a soup kitchen. She needed to be the vehicle of miracles in the world, instead of bemoaning the lack of miracles in her own life.

The change was dramatic. Suddenly her life had direction and purpose. She had been sent to do something. From her own loss of faith, she made goodness. She has decided to train for a life in charitable work.

Faith is how we set ourselves in the world. A famous incident in World War I was the Germans' sinking of the British steamer *Lusitania*. The ship carried some 2,000 people, more than half of whom drowned. The captain of that ship, William Turner, was watching his ship sink, knowing the certain fate of the passengers. He needed to say something, in a moment, that would summarize a lifetime of meaning and tell them how he, as the captain, expected them to conduct themselves. There was no time for long speeches. He looked out at the passengers and in a clear, loud voice said, "Be British." In those two words was a world. They knew what was expected of them. They shared an orientation to something greater than themselves. With faith, with trust in something "greater than," we magnify that message. Great hardships in human lives do not become calamitous until they undermine faith. Viktor Frankl recounted this tremendous realization in *Man's Search for Meaning*. In the concentration camps, Frankl realized that surviving meant believing. Those who could no longer hold on to some sort of faith collapsed inside and died. He developed a therapy based on getting the client to help other people. In moving out of themselves, the clients found the strength to search for and find meaning in their lives.

But believing does not mean steady certainty. Believing means not despairing of the worthiness of the search. Today, God may seem far. The world may seem drained, empty. Faith is the confidence that the search is not futile. An astronomer may scour the night sky not because he believes in the certainty of this or that star, but because he knows that diligent searching will yield something. "If someone says 'I searched and did not find,' do not believe him," says the Talmud. Perhaps the Talmud is trying to say that searching is the aim, and to honestly search is to show already that one has faith.

Rabbi Nachman of Bratzlav said that he was "a moon man— my faith waxes and wanes." The moon promises presence, and then days later it is gone. The losses, the valleys in between these peak moments, have to be crossed with the realization that the spiritual ground of life is not even. God sometimes will be inaccessible to us. Yet losing faith can be integral to having faith. Believing entails doubting. The moon waxes and wanes. The systolic/diastolic pattern found in the beating heart is present in the spirit. Without contraction, no expansion. Without loss, no attainment.

Growing in faith means learning its resiliency and complexity. We hold it before us as a simple, fragile vase that, once dropped, is irretrievably shattered. When faith is placed in the wrong arena, it is indeed fragile. We lose faith in people, in projects, in politicians. These are subsidiary faiths. Their loss is painful but inevitable. Ultimately faith finds its character not in one's trust of another, but in one's attitude toward the universe. Faith is a sinewy, complicated creation, capable of swelling and subsiding. Divine inspiration can pass, but the passing of one moment does not mean the end of the friendship. Deep faith is tough and lasting. It is durable enough to outlast even its own periodic absence.

Through the pages of the Bible we see God gradually recede: from the active, miracle-generating God of Genesis and Exodus to the all but undetectable God of later books such as Esther. We are not the first who have struggled. Our imagined ancestors, filled with faith, no doubt existed. But so did ancestors very much like ourselves, anxious, uncertain, searching.

The Baal Shem Tov once was approached by a man who had lost faith. God seemed far more distant than God had in his youth. The Baal Shem Tov replied that such a distance was natural. When children are young, we teach them to walk by standing beside them and holding their hands. As they grow, however, we gradually distance ourselves so that they can learn to walk to us. God has moved away, said the Baal Shem Tov, so that you might now learn how to walk on your own to God.

What if God's presence in the world is like a parent's presence in our lives? Perhaps God's was once more active, the world brighter with the imminence of the Divine. But as a child grows, a parent intervenes less. Closeness remains, concern endures, but autonomy demands that the individual, the human being, be allowed to make choices. If everything is God, if God indeed ordains every sparrow and moderates every movement, what room is there for being human?

Only by God permitting space for human beings to grow can humanity thrive. If our sole task is submission, we are mere puppets. But that is not the way we were created. If our capacities are to flower in this world, God's intervention must diminish.

To put the matter differently, unless we pull up the anchor of God's constant presence, we cannot sail. The weight of Divinity is too massive to allow our poor ships to make their way. But pulling up the anchor leaves us uneasily adrift. Self-reliance is dependent on distance, on the certainty that we can make our way unaided. With self-reliance comes hiddenness. We are not looking for God at each step.

God has granted us imperfect souls and a broken world. Our task is to burnish those souls and through them to make the world we have been given better. The meaninglessness that afflicts us is the doubt not only of God's place in the world—or of the existence of God—but of the aim of life.

The teaching that we have been made in the image of God does not tell us anything about our physical selves or that we are perfect. An image is not a replica. Being formed in the image of God means that there is in us the infinite capacity for growth, that we can never exhaust our ability to stretch ourselves spiritually.

Sometimes it is only later that we discover God's presence. The theologian Abraham Joshua Heschel taught that God speaks slowly in our lives, a syllable at a time. It is not until we reach the end of life, he said, that we can read the sentence backward. To find God later, perhaps we must lose God earlier.

In my own life I am grateful for the years I lived removed from religion. It allowed me to breathe, to return to my tradition a freer man. I spent a year in Scotland and walked only once, briefly, into a synagogue. I spent far more time marveling at castles and cathedrals, at museums and forests as I traveled through Europe. Looking back, I realize there were times of faith then, too, as now there are periods of dark doubt. One morning with some friends, I climbed Arthur's Seat, a jutting peak near the University of Edinburgh dormitories where I lived. We sat there, in silence, as the sun rose and the dawn broke over the city. It was not so much an experience of God as it was an experience of myself as a person of faith. I could not look at that site as interesting or beautiful alone. It was grand, climactic in some way. It spoke a truth about the world. We are small, but we are part of something so much larger, so much more grand and glorious than I allowed myself to imagine day by day. It took my breath away.

In later years I would return to that moment, and to a time when I took a bus across the United States. I was seventeen, and as we drove through the Colorado Rockies and I looked at the sculpted grandeur, I felt the presence of a shaping hand. I was a pretty resolute atheist, but in both instances I put aside what I thought and was swept up in what I felt, in what gripped me. In each case, the mountains seemed to dwarf the smallness of my certainties. In later years, the remembrance of those moments nourished me.

Heschel wrote, "Man was the first to hide himself from God, after having eaten of the forbidden fruit, and is still hiding. The will of God is to be here, manifest and near; but when the doors of this world are slammed on Him, His truth betrayed, His will defied, He withdraws, leaving man to himself. God did not depart of His own volition; he was expelled. God is in exile."

Heschel was convinced that God is waiting to emerge, hoping at each instant that humanity will beckon Him forward: "The prophets do not speak of the hidden God but of the hiding God. His hiding is a function not His essence, an act not a permanent state. It is when the people forsake Him, breaking the Covenant which He has made with them, that He forsakes them and hides His face from them. It is not God who is obscure. It is man who conceals Him." For Heschel, when we allow our wonder at the world to wane, when we seal up our hearts, we push God away.

In the book of Jeremiah, God says, "My soul weeps in secret places" (bamistarim). Commenting on this verse, the Rebbe of Mezhibozh told the following tale.

This can be explained by what happened to me and my grandchild. He asked me to play hide-and-seek with him, and I agreed. I closed my eyes and counted, and he went to hide. I was suddenly distracted by a friend and forgot all about the child. Soon I heard him crying from his hiding place, "No one has come to look for me." So does God cry, "I am hidden, and my children do not search for Me."

The Zohar speaks of "children from the chamber of yearnings." I feel that I am from that place. I want more than I can know. I seek sometimes without even knowing what I am seeking. We are children, all of us, who claim we want the peace of certainty but cannot seem to give up on the restlessness of searching.

When I pray, I try to break my heart. I think of the sadnesses of the world. I try to understand the ego that keeps me from God. As I child, when I was taught to pray, I learned the words and the gestures, but I missed the kernel, the heart of prayer. Prayer is not about the accuracy of the ritual but about offering up one's heart. It is not that God, or the world, needs one's heart, but that we need to be able to offer. Through recalling ancient altars upon which sacrifices were given to God, we seek to reopen our souls. The modern altar is the human soul, where we offer up our gratitude and sadness. Prayer is the moment when we agree not to hide.

Even the most faithful can feel a loss of faith.

Elie Wiesel once told a story of the *shammes* (synagogue sexton) who day after day, in the midst of the transports to the concentration camps, would go to the front of the synagogue and say, "Master of the Universe, I want you to know, we are still here." When he was finally left alone in the town, he went to the synagogue again, banged his fist, and said, "Master of the Universe, I want you to know, I am still here." And then he stopped, only to murmur, "But You—where are You?"

At times, God seems hidden or in eclipse. When we imagine an eclipse, we visualize something interposed between the sun and earth—or between God and humanity. The human hand is a tiny thing, but held before one's eyes it can block the sun. There are things we do that block faith, that keep us from entertaining the possibility that the world is a miracle. We become shackled by habit, by fear, by routines that contribute to a deadening of soul. Even religion itself can be destructive of faith when it becomes a sequence of rites without meaning.

How many times have I seen religious practice that is empty? How many times have I practiced without attention?

Each year of life can be like a tree ring; it adds a circle to our souls but moves us farther from the center. Things we were certain of recede, and visions cloud up. God, beauty, wonder—all were once smooth and natural. When we were children, faith was not an achievement, the way it seems now in adulthood. It was a gift, a natural endowment. As we grow, faith is not exactly gone, but it is hidden. No longer the constant accompaniment of our days, it is the searching we do at night.

An eclipsed God is a supremely inaccessible God. The paradox of faith is that in that inaccessibility, in that place where it seems we cannot reach, we sometimes find God. God is found in darkness, in cloud.

The Jewish calendar is gauged by the moon, not by the sun. In an interesting twist on Rabbi Nachman, who saw the waxing and waning moon as symbolic of his own struggle with faith, another commentator, the Sefat Emeth, argued that a lunar calendar is a sign of faith. The new month is declared when the moon is at its ebb. When the night is darkest, wrote the Sefat Emeth, we declare belief in the month to come. "One who sees the new moon is as one who sees God's presence." Having waited out the days of darkness, there is again light.

The moon has no light of its own. To rely on its illumination is a double act of faith—the moon emerges out of the darkness, and it is lit by an unseen source. That is why in mystical imagery, the moon represents the Divine presence. One cannot see God directly, but the Divine presence in the world is visible in flashes and hints. At times it appears in its fullness, as does the moon. At times faith flashes through us, but its source is beyond us.

The night is a time of faith and a time of doubt. The moon is an inconstant companion. When the sparkling distractions of the day settle, hearts can sometimes find their aims. The dark can be calming. But for many the night is a time of anxiousness, where wisps of memory jostle with ghosts of imagination; a fearful brew of regret and distress.

Still the picture becomes more complex, more subtly shaded as we grow. What we really want of God is less clear. Should the world be an untroubled paradise? John Keats wrote in one of his most famous letters: "Do you not see how necessary a World of Pains and Troubles is to school an intelligence and make it a Soul?" If life is a moral drama, can that drama have worth if there is no pain, no suffering, no overcoming? If our aim is to grow our souls, to climb spiritual rungs one by one, are we not better off with the adversity that forces us to climb? Could we possibly be anything more than puppets and robots if we lived on a perfect planet?

When I was a child, I used to watch "Star Trek." Many of the plots were repetitive: They land on a planet where there is no pain, but also no growth; the crew has to decide—should they stay there and be in a state of ignorant bliss forever, or leave and brave the turbulence of life? Of course, they always brave the turbulence—otherwise there is no episode for next week. But the underlying message is more serious. It is the same message one gets from Utopian novels where drugs or strict social control offer the same blissful emptiness. The hero is the one who will not settle for the pleasure that blocks out the drama and struggle and pain of life. Without pain there is no music, art, literature. Similarly, almost no science or technology would exist, because needs and pain are so closely related that to be without pain is to virtually be without need. You miss someone you love; you seek shelter from the elements, medicine for an ailment, relief from boredom in a novel or a movie, an expression of the angst in your soul that only music can give, a need to express what is bottled up inside you, a religious rite to bind up the wounds of your loss, a pillow for your tired head, and food for your empty stomach. Dealing with pain and expressing joy together create civilization. Perhaps God ought to have created a painless world, but it could not be with human beings.

Our souls are our unique endowment. Struggle is the leavening element of life. Through it we rise.

We yearn for God in a world spun out of control, and yet we doubt the reality of God. In the seed of our doubting there can be found faith. But the faith we find there is different from faith as we usually conceive of it. We think of the doubter as lost, but equally the believer can be lost—lost in impregnable pieties of one kind or another.

Faith is not a fortress. We are not locked into it. I do not believe as I did ten years ago, and I hope I do not believe today as I will ten years from now. My faith has become more honest as I have grown. But it is not easy.

Losing faith is a universal experience. Things we loved are not as we believed them to be. Bitter from losing, we can become skeptical.

If we can admit our disillusion and believe it is not the end of the search, we can move forward. My advice to people who have lost faith is not to lose faith in faith. Don't believe that because faith is sometimes hard it has fled forever. Have faith in the searching. Loss is the platform on which we build a deeper, sturdier faith.

But every time, every time I speak about finding one's way back to God, I hear that same voice, the voice of the child in the orphanage saying, "My mommy told me never to let go of his hand," the voice of the one who says, "What about me? What about the world that God created that I was born into only to suffer?" and I know that it's not allowed to be easy. There are people who have told me that they never doubted their faith in God no matter what they faced. I envy that certainty. It is not mine. For me it is a struggle, and in some ways I cannot keep faith with that child if I don't struggle, if I don't wonder, if I don't doubt, if I don't pray, not only to ask of God but to find God.

Right before the High Holidays, a congregant, a lovely woman named Hannah Lippert, well into her nineties, brought in an editorial that Elie Wiesel had written in the *New York Times* about his encounter with God some fifty years after the end of the Holocaust. Wiesel wrote, " 'What about my faith in You, master of the universe?' I now realize that I never lost it, not even over there during the darkest hours of my life." Wiesel closed his beautiful meditation as follows: "As we Jews now enter the High Holidays again preparing ourselves to pray for a year of peace and happiness for our people and all people, let us make up, master of the universe, in spite of everything that has happened, yes in spite, let us make up for the child in me, it is unbearable to be divorced from You for so long."

I did not become a rabbi because I believe. I became a rabbi because I committed my life to never giving up searching and yearning for God. I am a rabbi because there is in me, as there is in you, a child, a child that knows that somewhere we are not alone; that this world is bathed in miracles; and that for every pain there is beauty, for every loss there is love, and for every waste there is wonder.

I continue to seek God because I know this is the human task. I seek, because in that search there is life, and light, and meaning, and even joy.

There is indeed joy in faith, and joy in the quest for faith. The world often cooperates if we see in it the beauty that awaits. Sanctity dwells in everything that exists. Wielded as a spiritual sword, a blade of grass is a lever sturdy enough to pry open the gate to holiness.

Faith is not only an earnest search, it is a dance. One who believes in the ultimate goodness of the universe will not necessarily be happy, but joy is deeper than happiness. Joy does not obviate loss. When we lose faith, we have a chance to pull ourselves higher, and often the rung that we can grasp is the rung of joy.

The Kotzker Rebbe taught that God fashioned a ladder that reaches from heaven to earth, and on this ladder souls climb down in order to be born. When we reach earth, the ladder is drawn up and we are told to get back to heaven. Most give up because there is no ladder. Some leap but quickly become discouraged. Others leap and leap, knowing that if God sees leaping souls, He will reach down in mercy and lift them up to Him. Among those who struggle with faith, some remain earthbound, and others become leaping souls.

Seven

Life

"My father is dead?" I said. "What does that mean?"

"That means you won't see him again."

"But how? I won't see Father again?"

"No."

"And why shan't I see him again?"

"Because God has taken him back from you."

"Forever?"

"Forever."

"And you say I shan't see him again?"

"Never again."

"Never again, never?"

"Never!"

"And where does God live?"

"He lives in the sky."

I remained thoughtful for a while. Though such a child, and unable to reason, I understood nevertheless that something final had happened in my life. Then, seizing the first moment when nobody was paying attention to me, I escaped from my uncle's house and ran straight to my mother's.

All the doors were open, all the faces showed distress. Death could be sensed there.

I entered without being noticed. I reached a small room where arms were kept; I took down a single-barreled gun which belonged to my father, and which had often been promised me when I grew up.

Then, armed with the gun, I went upstairs.

*On the first floor I met my mother. She was coming out of the death chamber . . .
she was in tears.*

*"Where are you going?" she asked, astonished to see me there when she thought I
was with my uncle.*

"I'm going to the sky!" I answered.

"What, you are going to the sky?"

"Yes, don't stop me."

"And what are you going to do in the sky, my poor child?"

"I'm going to kill God, who killed Father."

       —*Alexandre Dumas* (1802–70), My Memoirs

I first encountered death when I was five years old. My great-aunt, my grandmother's sister, Bessie, died in Boston after a brief illness. Bessie never had children. She and her husband helped raise my father, an only child, after his father died. So my brothers and I were the children in Bessie's life, and she loved us. She used to tell my father, and her sister, my grandmother, that there would be no one to remember her when she was gone.

When she died, my family made the trip up to Boston. I have a few memories of that trip. I was devastated, but I did not know why. I remember going into Bessie's bedroom to cry. Soon after, my father entered the room. He told me that sometimes when we are crying for someone who died, we are not crying for them but really for ourselves, because we will miss them. At the time it did not seem right to me. I was crying for the terrible thing that had happened to Bessie. I could not untangle the sorrow. I knew only that something very important had been taken away.

Of course, something invaluable had been taken. It was not only Bessie, who loved me because I was named for her late husband, who even loved the faces I made that annoyed my grandmother. It was my sense of comfortable permanence. The world was far less stable than I knew, than I could have imagined. If Aunt Bessie could die . . .

We all went to the funeral. I don't remember the service itself, but I remember the aftermath. We stood before the open grave. My grandmother wept bitterly, howlingly. Suddenly, my grandmother tried to throw herself into Bessie's grave. Bessie was her older sister, older by some eleven years. She was losing a sister, a mother, the chord that bound her childhood to her present. I did not understand any of those things at the time. All I knew was that my grandmother, an old woman in my eyes, someone far beyond the reach of unrestrained feeling, was trying to throw herself into an open grave.

The ground seemed omnivorous. It had swallowed Aunt Bessie, and now it was threatening to swallow up my grandmother. Only my parents' restraining her prevented it. My grandmother was generally a very calm, almost detached woman. In all the years I knew her—and she lived well into my adulthood—she was never given to frenzied bouts of emotion. She rarely got angry, rarely seemed buoyant with joy. Even as a child I perceived this evenness and how it contrasted with the behaviors of other adults I knew. Her reaction was not some dramatic dance step to be expected from an hysteric. It was the unspeakable anguish of loss, played out before all of us in a private, small drama whose chorus repeats endlessly in life. My parents' preventing her from throwing herself in seemed unfair to me, in a way. I knew they were doing the right thing, the thing that would prove wise in the long run. At the moment, however, falling into the grave was the truthful act, the one that kept faith with the awfulness of the moment. It taught me how we forsake immediate pain in order to survive. We often are untrue to ourselves this way. We will not smash a plate, scream in agony, run off the road, because we know that the acute pang of loss is in the now and that life will provide some solace in time. Still, the solace is a betrayal of the grief, one we should not ignore. Surely for the rest of her life, my grandmother remembered Bessie's open grave and wondered why she did not at that moment have the strength to force her way in there.

By being untrue in this way, we are true to the deeper reality of loss. By enduring, we make a statement that even the most poignant loss can be made meaningful. Refusing to succumb to despair is the greatest act of faith. We may despair for a moment. Darkness seems ascendant. We cry out. But stirring within is the certainty that the pain of a particular loss is a sign of having loved. Where the capacity to love has been, it can be again.

The world spins, but we do not feel it. Time moves, and we do not realize it. No matter how meticulously we mark off the instants into days, months, and years, we still are surprised when we look back at the distance that has accumulated behind us. It is suddenly appalling that so much time has gathered behind us, appalling because we are aware of our certain destination.

Death is a loss unlike any other because it embraces everything. When we die, we lose all the earthly things we know: music and mountains, family and books, food and wine, walks and sunsets, newspapers and sports and movies and friends and love. In a brief poem by A. E. Housman, a man standing in a town square threatens suicide. His words describe not only his own death but, paradoxically, the end of the world.

Good people, do you love your lives
And have you ears for sense?
Here is a knife like other knives
That cost me eighteen pence.
I need but plunge it in my heart
And down will come the sky
And earth's foundations will depart
And all you folk will die.

The enormity of life's ending hovers over all our doings in this world. Death is the culmination of losses. The ancient book of Ecclesiastes expresses how death makes a mockery of achievement in this world: "For in respect to the fate of man and the fate of beast, they have one and the same fate: as the one dies so dies the other, and both have the same life breath; man has no superiority over beast, since both amount to nothing. Both go to the same place; both come from dust and both return to dust. . . . [T]he race is not won by the swift, nor the battle by the valiant; nor is bread won by the wise, nor wealth by the intelligent, nor favor by the learned. For time and chance comes to all" (3:19–21; 9:11).

The greatest single fact about existence is its reality—that it is. Short steps behind that first great truth is that existence is temporary. Whatever else life's characteristics, one thing we always know is that life does not last.

For centuries, students began learning logic with a simple

syllogism: "Socrates is a man; all men are mortal; therefore Socrates is mortal." The Spanish philosopher Unamuno wrote that the real syllogism underneath this is: "I am a man; all men are mortal; therefore I will die."

As we get older, we realize the suddenness with which death looms over life. We always know it is there, but suddenly we wake up and something is wrong; suddenly the doctor calls to talk about our tests. Life swings on a hinge, reversing in an instant.

That we will die is not the conscious guiding principle of each day. Only the morbid spend all their time thinking about death, for to think only of death is paralyzing. One who contemplates death alone cannot live. But death is real, omnipresent, gliding just beneath the surface of being.

In the course of my lecturing, I frequently find myself on airplanes. I am not afraid to fly. I will eat, read, sleep, watch a movie, work. I stare out the window and marvel at the passing clouds. Flying has become routine. Apart from periodically being amazed that we are actually hurtling through space in a metal tube, and having gratitude for living in an age when such wonders exist, I do not think much about the trip. I am settled, calm, not afraid to fly.

But everything changes when the plane hits turbulence. As the rocking begins, there is a sudden surge of adrenaline. My fingers grip the seat. I cannot concentrate on the book before me. I feel the brush of mortality on my cheek. It does not matter that this is the same rocking I have felt many times before. It does not matter that the chances are infinitesimal that such shaking represents anything serious. I cannot help it; the grip of fear is deeper than my reason, more rooted than experience. I look around to see if others seem calm or unsettled by the shaking. My equanimity is undone.

At such times I realize that I am indeed afraid to fly. It is unnerving to be 30,000 feet up in the air with no control over one's own destiny. It matters little how safe flying is reputed to be; statistics cannot argue with panic in the gut.

The fear of flying exists in me, but it lies well below the surface, ready to explode when shaken loose. So it is with the fear of death. Seemingly absent, fear erupts when life hits turbulence. When we are sick, when someone close to us is dying, when we discover obituaries of people younger then ourselves, we feel everything from the twinge of discomfort to the flat-out dread of living in a world that does not promise permanence.

As with all losses, the first question is, Do we admit them? Or do we deny their reality in our lives? Death is real, but many of us live as if it cannot happen to us or to those whom we love. Part of our task is to feel its reality and learn from the loss that is most encompassing, the loss of life.

In the Jewish burial ceremony, the family is urged to shovel dirt on the coffin of the deceased. The thud of dirt on the coffin is blunt, even brutal. It jolts the heart. Hearing it impresses upon those who survive that this is real. Someone is being placed in the ground and will not return.

Families often recoil from this concluding ritual. I gently encourage them to participate by pointing out that this is a kindness they can do for the departed—one that otherwise will be done by strangers. But the deeper intent is a kindness not only to the dead but to the living. The beginning of renewed life is to absorb the reality of death.

Modern society insulates us from death. Death is hidden in a thousand ways. We die behind closed hospital doors. Those who eat meat do not see the animal slaughtered. Death is far more likely to be seen on the movie screen than in life—and on the screen we know that the actor really has not died. The earth hits the coffin, and death is real, visceral, permanent.

To acknowledge death is not to approve of the design of the world. Acknowledging death does not resolve the question of whether death is an unredeemable loss, or, as with the other losses of life, it may be turned to good.

The plot of William Trevor's short story "Death in Jerusalem" turns upon a death. Two brothers—Father Paul, a priest, and Francis, a simple, devoted, and pious man—are visiting Jerusalem. While they are there, their mother dies in her small town back home in Ireland. The death makes Francis hate the holy land forever. He should have been home. But the same death cuts Father Paul's ties to home forever. Same loss, different losses. One death, two legacies.

The person who dies had many different identities in life and is mourned differently by each one who is left behind. For one person, the deceased is an old friend, for another a father, for another a brother, for a third a son. The losses reverberate through the twists of memory and time. Even when the role is the same, the personal experience is different. While I was writing this book, my father's best friend from childhood died. When my father and I spoke on the phone, he told me how a bit of his childhood was now irrevocably lost. Cy was someone who did not treat my father as a rabbi; he was a friend. He would call my father and sing old camp songs. Now that those songs are stilled, part of my father's past is gone. In "Death in Jerusalem," both Francis and Paul lose a mother, but the mother represents something different for each of them. We generalize about death, but it wears a unique guise for each survivor. The Baal Shem Tov, the founder of Hasidism, once remarked that there are no doubles. No two people are alike; no two moments are alike. He might have said no two deaths are alike.

During the year I spent in Scotland, some friends and I decided to take a trip to the northern part of the country. There we hitchhiked, slept in people's backyards, pitched tents on public golf courses, and walked in the freezing drizzle of the highlands. Part of the trip was taken up by an excursion to the famous loch, or lake, that is reputed to be the home of the Loch Ness monster.

On our way there we walked by the side of the road. An older lady in a broken-down car stopped and encouraged us to climb in. We were grateful for the ride, and spoke about her life and our travels. As we approached the lake, she suddenly stopped the car, got out, and asked me if I would drive.

I was puzzled, but I agreed, and we began to drive by the famous lake. I asked her why she wanted me to drive. "I always try to sit by the window that faces the loch. I was married for almost fifty years," she said, "and my husband was a great believer in the monster—a great believer. Myself, I never believed it—thought it was all nonsense." She paused. "But now that he is gone," she said, "I watch the loch for him."

Death reminds us of the other losses of life. When we mourn for a person, we also mourn for the time that is gone, the places we shared, the world we once inhabited together. Soldiers stand at the funeral of their compatriot and cry not only for the one they have lost but for the loss of youth, of shared purpose, of noble hours. The world rarely steals away but one thing at a time.

In Jewish tradition, when a relative dies, the family "sits *shiva*"—literally "seven." For one week, various rites of mourning are observed. It is called "sitting *shiva*" because the mourner traditionally sits on a low stool to enact the feeling of being brought low by grief. The family gathers together and remembers the deceased. Friends visit and pay respects. Part of the rites of *shiva* consist in covering the mirrors of the household. There has been a loss of the Divine image in the world, embodied in the human face. Not only are mirrors symbols of inappropriate vanity at a time of grief, but not to look at one's face reminds us that the world has been diminished because one image of God, an image like ourselves, is gone.

Shiva teaches that loss is formless and grief must be shaping. Loss, a deep loss, is chaotic, cavernous; it resounds in the hollows of the soul. It rages, and nothing can tame it. Ritual seeks to give us order and structure. Understanding what we have lost, we can find a place for the memory inside us.

A friend once explained to me his experience of sitting *shiva*. He told me that during the week that he was mourning the death of his parent, he was resolved not to call his office. When coworkers came by to offer condolences, he did not talk about what was going on at the office and deliberately turned the conversation aside when they began "shop talk."

When the week of mourning ended, he immediately called the office, only to discover that everything was fine. He realized then that *shiva* is a way of preparing for one's own death. It reinforces the painful truth—the world will get along without me. The office will run, the stars will glint, and the earth will spin. The graveyards are full of indispensable people.

A legend teaches that the first night Adam lived through after his creation, he was terrified. The light and warmth had gone out of the garden, and he did not understand what was happening. Having never experienced darkness before, he could not know that the sun would rise again. The world seemed permanently plunged into blackness and danger. God instructed him to rub together two stones, and fire was first seen on earth. The two stones had names: *afelah* and *mavet*, darkness and death.

Asked once what he would save if his house should catch on fire, the Kotzker Rebbe answered, "I would take the spark that began the flame."

Destruction and loss bear within them a spark. To hold the spark while still letting go of what has been lost is an essential human task.

When we face death, we face the possibility of meaninglessness. The crux of living is to believe that this loss can be a spur to radiance.

Experience is the name we give to the enforced learning of life. One of the grand aims of education is to give us the lessons of experience without the pain.

The holiest day of the year in the Jewish calendar, Yom Kippur, is the day of atonement, and the day of death. It is on that day that we confront the reality of our own deaths. Yom Kippur is designed to teach us how to do that by enacting a drama in symbolic, ritual ways.

The traditional garb on Yom Kippur is a white robe. White is a sign of purity; as one scholar remarks, we wear white because it shows the slightest stain. More deeply, it recalls the *tachrichin*, the shrouds in which a person is buried. On Yom Kippur, we imagine ourselves as if we had died.

We do not eat. We do not wash. We are corpses. The harshness of that reality leads many to shrink from it. But Yom Kippur teaches that if we cannot envision what it is to die, we will not be able to savor life and to live it well.

The most famous prayer of Yom Kippur, Unetaneh Tokef, is a brutal recapitulation of the starkness of mortality: "Who shall live and who shall die?" Because the prayer is recited but once a year, the congregation will inevitably look around for those who were present and praying last year but who are now gone. They too recited those words, not knowing that the coming year would claim them for death. The message is that mortality is wanton, capricious; death can strike anyone. It could strike me.

"Who shall die by fire, and who by water, who by sword, and who by wild beast; who by famine, and who by thirst, who by strangling, and who by stoning . . ." The words are specific and tied to the medieval age in which they were written. Substitute modern terms: "Who by heart attack, and who by car crash; who by AIDS, and who by cancer; who by neglect, and who by despair . . ." The immediacy of the prayer brings home the solemnity of the day.

The Unetaneh Tokef tells us that we do not have forever. Loss is not an incidental accompaniment to life; it is life's recurrent, urgent motif. Live with your eye on eternity and your foot fixed on the shifting sand, and forget neither one.

One year on Yom Kippur, a woman in my congregation who had been quite sick could not attend services. Linda had been in and out of the hospital for weeks, and her prognosis was uncertain at best. It was the first time since she was an infant that she had not been in synagogue on Yom Kippur. She told me afterward that the words of the prayer kept ringing in her head. What would be her fate this year? Who will live, and who will die? Was the prayer speaking to her? Would she be here next year to return to the synagogue?

We talked for a long time. Finally I said to her, "Linda, I know you are afraid. What are you going to do with your fear?" "Well, Rabbi," she answered, "I am going to live with the fear, and I am going to *really* live in spite of it."

King David was a poet and a warrior, the most vibrant of all biblical figures. Throughout the books of Samuel, we see in David a man filled with the zest and brio of life. Yet when we open the first book of Kings, David is an old man, shivering in bed, and he cannot even keep himself warm. The first verse reads: "King David was now old, advanced in years." One chapter later, the Bible reads, "David was dying" (2:1). The Rabbis noticed a significant difference in those two verses. When he is old, he is still called King David. When he is dying, he is simply David.

When it comes to death, said the philosopher Epicurus, we all live in an unwalled city. No one is protected, and the futility of evasion makes our attempts to deny it desperate and doomed. Living in Los Angeles, I am sometimes reminded that the philosophy of the city is reflected in the seasons. In L.A. there is no autumn. People do not wish to age. They want to be young up to the day they die. Aging, with its insinuation of the end, is terrifying to the city of illusions. We can hide behind power and position and title in this world. But we face our own deaths as children, stripped of the disguises of the world.

Denying death is not only futile—the sociologist Simmel compares fleeing before death to a person on a boat who walks the deck in the opposite direction to the vessel, thinking he is reversing course—it also blocks life. Fear robs us of freedom. We cannot embrace the beauty of the world if we are always checking the mirror and our own pulse. The terror of loss is more debilitating than the loss itself.

Understanding that we can make loss meaningful is not the same as being glad that loss happened. Shaking our fists at the sky, filled with anger and bewilderment, is not inconsistent with trying to use loss as a ladder for growth. Rabbi Harold Kushner, author of *When Bad Things Happen to Good People*, has made the searing remark that the loss of his child has made him a better person, a better rabbi, a wiser and more compassionate man— and he would give it all back in an instant if he could have his child back.

When a person moves through this world, however briefly, he leaves a trail. We crisscross one another's lives, leaving traces of influence, of meaning. Each of us brings something, even if at first we cannot figure out precisely what it is that we mean to one another. Sometimes we are so involved in our own lives that we cannot step back from the canvas to see the picture.

When parents lose a child, it is their task to understand how the child's life had purpose. The purpose is not only intrinsic but created. In other words, each person's life has meaning simply by virtue of carrying his or her own Divine spark into the world. But also we help create meaning for the lives who touch us. When we change our lives because someone else has changed us or moved us, we create meaning for the other person's life as well.

Part of the powerful magic of life is that we never know when we touch other people or change their lives. In our own lives, we remember things that others said to us or did for us—things that they probably do not remember and did not recognize as being important at the time.

When I was thirteen, I attended a summer camp in the Pocono Mountains in Pennsylvania. I did not want to go. I was unhappy being told what to do, where to go, how to live. I was confused about life, sexuality, self-worth, and just about everything else. I was a smart aleck and a pain in the neck.

But I remember one incident from that summer. Right before bedtime, I was standing on the porch of my cabin. Everyone else was inside, playing cards, laughing, enjoying themselves, while I was looking at the stars, wrapped up in a bout of self-pity. My counselor, whom I liked very much, came out and stood beside me. We talked for a minute, and then suddenly he told me he had a choice of two colleges to attend that fall. He asked me where I thought he should go.

That question was an extraordinary gift. I was being taken seriously, asked to give advice on something I knew nothing about, just because he valued my opinion. Today I don't know whether he used this strategy to snap me out of my funk or he really cared to hear what I had to say, but at the time, my world was changed. More than twenty years later, I have not forgotten. To someone I respected, I was far from worthless.

Lives can be most powerfully changed at vulnerable moments. A life can take a turn at any time, but there are special times—what sociologists call liminal moments—which open wide the door to transformation. When death strikes, people are in shock at first. But the loss changes things and leaves people in a fluid state. Soon people's outlooks, like heated glass, become pliable and ready to assume new shapes. If they can create meaning from the life of the person who has died, they can reshape their own lives. Something in the legacy of the deceased might move the survivors to change themselves or to commemorate the one who has died. Perhaps a lesson from his life crystallizes and has renewed force now that he is gone. Meaning is rarely confined to one; in giving another meaning, we share it in our own lives as well.

Such was the case with a couple I know who lost a very young child. The key to their life became finding what could grow from that empty place. They explored more deeply both their faith and their love.

Why did it happen? What had become of their child after death? By asking those questions, they began the process of making meaning, for meaning begins in questioning. The one who does not search will not find. The one who does not search will lose anew, for he will have lost not only the person but the complex of meanings and the richness of memory that the person leaves behind.

In time, those questions received not answers but newer formulations, greater understanding. The couple thought of how their child should be commemorated. What did his life really mean? How had he touched them? What was his legacy?

Their faith was not unwavering, and it did not erase the pain. Each day is still a trial. But their faith is real, though not expressed in prayer or declarations alone. Their faith was expressed in a simple gesture: They had another child.

When we read a book, the pages diminish. We can look ahead and see how far we ought to go. In that sense, no book can reproduce life, because we know the terminus. Life does not grant that knowledge; the story could end today or in fifty years. Yet age is the visible sign of the dwindling pages. Where once we had counted on an unbounded future, now we begin to number the years.

Every week I study with a gentleman who is in his eighties. He is vigorous and alert, but he hears "time's winged chariot hurrying near." From time to time when we study, he will suddenly mention his expectation that his life will soon end. He looks at the progress we have made studying each session, and then shakes his head. He wishes he had started studying sooner. One day as I left his front door, he called after me: "Rabbi, don't forget that we're scheduled for Thursday. There is a lot left to do, and the sun is setting."

The last several years have not been easy for him. He was in a terrible accident that laid him up for months. Then he suffered a stroke that robbed him of fluent speech, though he can still speak clearly, if with deliberation and care. All along the path, there have been small losses that are flagstones laid down to a destination.

At the same time, he has suddenly become fascinated with questions that used to be unimportant to him. He is concerned about leaving a legacy. All that he has accomplished in his life is not enough, because as he sees misfortunes firsthand, he knows how easily other things are lost—accomplishments, memories. That which seems permanent passes away. So he wants to contribute more, build more playgrounds, ask more questions, meet more people, learn more, create anew.

One result of the stroke is that sometimes he is debilitatingly depressed. Some mornings uselessness drapes itself over him, making it hard for him to get out of bed. So much he once had is gone—ease of movement and speech, so many friends, some certainties.

He fights the depression with the faith that what he does matters. Religious study has helped shore up his belief that this world is not simple vanity, a passing away, a breath that disappears. Remarkably, as we turn the pages of the Bible together, he is revived by the thought that these men and women, who lived and cried and faltered thousands of years ago, still live in our memory and imagination. They glow, they inspire, they perplex. Because they lived deeply, loving the world but also looking beyond it, their life messages endure. When we close the book, after talking about life, loves, his experiences, the future and the past, the day seems lighter. When nothingness threatens, faith is the weapon of choice.

One of our recurrent conversations is about life after death. Is this world all there is?

My elderly friend and student says he does not believe in another world. He tells me people think he is studying religion because he is afraid of what will happen after death. "It's nonsense," he insists. "A fairy tale for the frightened." I find it equally hard to believe that all we are simply vanishes. I don't think we go to a physical place. After all, the essence, the soul, is not physical. As the Israeli scholar Adin Steinsaltz once remarked, to ask "where the soul goes is a nonsense question. The soul is not physical. Where does a dream go once it has been dreamt? Where does love go when it disappears?"

We cannot conceive of what life might be like if it is not material like this life. In this life we are tied to the tangible, except our deepest experiences tend to be things that are not really physical, like love, like memory. We cannot imagine what happens after death, but the poverty of our imagination does not prove that the world is not more creative than we know.

It is lovely to think that the loss of this world is a ticket price to the inheritance of the next. Maybe we step through this world as if through a corridor. A beautiful comment by Bronson Alcott, friend of Emerson and father of Louisa May Alcott, ties together the themes of failing memory and the world to come. As he grew older, Emerson started to lose his memory. He tried to get around it—once, forgetting the term "umbrella," he called it "the thing that strangers take away"—but it troubled him. He was consoled by Alcott, who made reference to the Platonic legend that human beings know all about this world but lose that knowledge the moment we are born. Likewise, he said that as we get older, we start to lose knowledge of this world in the form of failing memory, to prepare us for the next one. Each time we cannot remember something about this world, it is not a failing but a letting go.

This comment echoes a Jewish parable of the afterlife. The parable asks us to imagine two twins in the womb. One of them believes that the world inside the womb is not all. There must be another world, he argues; he believes in something unimaginable that he has never seen. Though he cannot possibly envisage mountains and lakes, giraffes and plums, he has faith in something greater than the womb-world of his experience.

His brother in the womb thinks such an idea preposterous. This is the only world we have ever known, he argues. Your faith in something greater is only an earnest wish. It is nonsense, and when we are through here, there is nothing more.

Now imagine that the one who believes is born. His brother back in the womb is mourning a death. But outside they are celebrating a birth. So it is with us on earth. As Alcott said, our final years here are not the end of all, but a preparation for the other world we will enter.

The most powerful and comprehensive attempt to ease the loss attendant upon death is the belief that we will live on. Believing in another world makes the losses of this world less enduring and more bearable. But of course we cannot be certain if there is another world. We are not granted a glimpse.

The idea that we continue takes many forms, from the existence of another world to the lightest, least concrete, which is that we live on in memory. The English poet James Elroy Flecker, who hoped to live on through the artistry of his lines addressed to a poet who will read them 1,000 years later, wrote: "O friend unseen, unborn, unknown, / Student of our sweet English tongue, / Read out my words at night, alone: / I was a poet, I was young."

The comfort of memory may be all we have. If so, then living well, creating art or children, is the only assurance of permanence, because then we will leave a legacy.

Leaving a legacy is a heroic ideal, one which we find in classical poetry and the Greek world from which it grew. In *The Iliad*, the martial legacy of Achilles endures, not the warrior himself. Achilles dies, but to die heroically and leave a memory shining to posterity is surely better than to eke out a few more miserable years as a coward. The same notion lives in the famous funeral oration of Pericles, in epic poems, in the encomiums lavished on heroism in *Plutarch's Lives*. As written in the medieval epic *Beowulf*: "We must all expect an end to life in this world; let him who can win fame before death, because that is a dead man's best memorial."

The ideal persists today. At funerals, we are told that "this person will live on in the memory of his good deeds, and in the hearts of those who love him." This sentiment helps with the loss, but it does not take it away. Still, the person is gone. Still the family is bereft. Still, there is a hole in the world.

The soft, insistent voice of something more whispers in our ear. Can this be all?

Undergirding all discussion of death is the howling unfairness of it all. Death is still so arbitrary, reaching all but at different times in different ways. Death's inevitability does not seem to soften, for most, the stinging reality that we have not tasted a fraction of the marvels the world has to offer—the love, the wonder, the stunning variety.

Unfairness is woven into the fabric of all life. Sometimes we are tempted to deny the unfairness. Religions fall into this trap.

They find ways to make the world fair. Believers in reincarnation will argue that we are born into the condition that we need to be in so that we might realize potentialities unfulfilled in previous lives. That this condemns those who exist in squalor and despair to the additional burden of *deserving* their condition (since their behavior in a previous life demands it) seems not to dampen enthusiasm for the theory.

Similar is the assumption that death comes when, and to whom, it is deserved. "It must have been his time" is the refrain of one who is loath to say that some people die before their time, whenever that might be. In the words of Pope, "Whatever is, is right." This belief gets God, or nature, or us off the hook for making this world so unfair.

I have seen people die who should not have died. I know this statement will strike some as arrogant—how can I know? Yet everything in me rebels against an easy acceptance. I remember a student of mine, a beautiful boy, curly haired and full of life, who died driving home from his sixteenth birthday party. He was loved, he was joyous, he was special. His death tore at the hearts of his family and his community. He died too soon.

How can I be reconciled to the death of a beautiful woman who battled cancer for several years before succumbing? Her children, three daughters and a son, watched her die. Her husband sat by her bed. She was good-natured, charitable, and well loved. Hundreds of people came to her funeral. She will not see her children's graduations or weddings. She died too soon.

Once I sat by the grave of a man a year after he died, talking about him with his widow. He left behind two young children, one of them disabled. He was a famous man, brilliantly talented, and all of it did not help him prevail against an illness that claimed his life in his early forties. His widow told me about his life, his spirit, his tremendous successes, his optimism, his hope until the very end. He will be remembered by the many whom he touched, but his children will not have a father, and his wife has lost the man who made her laugh. Who would say his time had come? Life is not fair.

That life is not fair is a powerful declaration that we are reluctant to accept. "That's not *fair*" is a cry every parent has heard. Children learn this painful truth early. The deepest impulses of the heart demand fairness, but the world has different plans. Each day noble people die too young, wicked people prosper, pestilence sweeps innocent populations, and the world spins on, indifferent to the anguish that blankets so much of the globe.

The history of suffering shapes the worldview of every faith. Anyone who looks back over human history cannot help but see that for all humanity's brilliance, the human countenance throughout the ages is elongated, deepened, and saddened, like the face in an El Greco painting. The lines are etched in grief, while the steady nobility of the eyes hints at something more.

In such a world, the secret of living is not to make loss worthwhile, but to make it meaningful. When Michael's widow and I sat on that grave and spoke of Michael's death, she was arranging his legacy, understanding what he had given her. She created a huge charity event in his memory to speed the cure of the cancer that had killed him. She tried to realize his spirit in her life.

When we think about those who have died, and try to understand their lives and teachings, we are permitting faith to shine through loss. Faith is not denying that the death was tragic; it is insisting that it can carry lessons, that it can bring meaning into the lives of those who remember.

What could we cherish were it forever? Would we hold babies so close with such heart-wringing fervor if we knew they would retain that wonderful smell and smooth skin and endearing embrace forever? Spring forever, without the bracing frame of fall, would not charm us. If we can grow bored or weary in a world of such delights, granted for such a brief time, what would we make of eternity?

All this reasoning does not dismiss our hopes. We still would choose more—more time, more life, more years, more love. Immortality must be good, proclaimed the Greek poet Sappho, or why would the gods choose it? We cannot still the longing for more.

In a beautiful passage opening his autobiography *Speak Memory*, Vladimir Nabokov wrote about the parallel between the time before we are born and the time after we die. He told of someone fearful of time, a chronophobiac, who sees home movies of his family before he was born and is disturbed by the recognition that no one missed him. He sees his cradle, the one in which he would soon be rocked and sung to, and it bears to him, "the smug, encroaching air of a coffin."

We know the world existed before us and will exist after. But we are not horrified by the time before we were born, for that time was not first given and then snatched away. It is the loss of what we have been given, not the objective state of death, that we fear. Life is measured by what we have had the chance to grasp. Traditionally in Judaism, birthdays are trivial, but a *yarzheit*, the anniversary of a person's death, is terribly important.

For a *yarzheit* is a symbol of the progress and achievements of a life, not simply years lived. A *yarzheit* is the symbol of defiance against death.

Memory is our defense against meaninglessness. My aunt Bessie feared being forgotten. I keep a photograph of her on my desk, next to a watch that belonged to her husband. Writing her name on this page was the best I could do to summon her memory and help her live on. It is so little. And yet many do not claim even that paltry memorial.

When a relative dies, Judaism prescribes that the mourner rip his or her garment. The tear in the universe is paralleled by the tear in the clothing covering the mourner. Mourners who have not yet cried often cry when the garment is torn. Yet in some ways, equally painful is when the torn garment is taken off. For then healing begins, which means that memory supplants grief. And grief—immediate, fresh, disbelieving grief—is far more potent than the threads of memory. Memory is recalling. While we grieve, we live in the moment of loss. As memory builds, the time of loss moves farther away.

When my grandfather was diagnosed with cancer, we knew that he soon would die. At the time, I was in Los Angeles and going away to spend the year in Israel. When I visited the East Coast, I saw him for what I knew would be the last time. As we looked at each other, there was an unspoken acknowledgment. There was a sadness in his eyes that I will always remember. Also, there was love.

I spoke silently to myself, "David, pay attention to what he looks like, how he feels, how he smells. Here is someone important in your life whom you will never see again." We kissed and cried. We hugged each other. Then he got into the car and my grandmother drove him away. As he was rounding the corner away from our house, I thought, *I am already losing him.*

Nothing is an adequate substitute for presence. And death steals presence. For that alone, it is difficult for us to forgive the design of this world.

My grandfather's death was not meaningless. He was loved by those who knew him, and his funeral was filled with people whose lives he had enriched by his easy, gentle presence. For although death is a great loss, the greater loss is to live trivially or meaninglessly. To live with faith and decency reduces the tragedy of death.

For the martyr, death is the lesser loss. Principle endures and overrides the individual's end. Socrates drank the hemlock because escaping the sentence would have contradicted the message of his life. He would rather die than be unfaithful to himself. For the Rabbis of the Talmud and later Jews who chose to continue practicing and teaching Judaism in the face of almost certain death, the loss of connection to God, to the tradition, and to their people far outweighed the loss from death.

The Talmud tells the stirring tale of the martyrdom of Rabbi Akiva.

> *Once the wicked government (the Romans) issued a decree forbidding Jews to teach Torah and practice their faith. Pappus ben Judah saw Rabbi Akiva publicly teaching Torah. Pappus said to him: "Akiva, aren't you afraid of the government?"*
>
> *Akiva answered: "I will explain our situation with a parable. Once a fox was walking alongside a river, and he saw fish swimming from one place to another. He said to them: 'From what are you fleeing?' They replied: 'From the*

fishermen's nets.' The fox said: 'Would you like to come up onto the dry land so that you and I can live together as my ancestors lived with your ancestors?' The fish replied: 'And they call you the cleverest of beasts? You are a fool! If we are frightened of being in the water, where we live, how much more frightened would we be to climb onto the dry land, where we die!'

"You see," said Akiva, "it is the same with us. If we are in trouble when we study Torah, imagine how much worse off we should be if we neglected our faith!"

Shortly afterward, Rabbi Akiva was arrested and thrown into prison, and Pappus ben Judah was also arrested and imprisoned next to him. Akiva said to him: "Pappus, why were you arrested?" Pappus replied: "Happy are you, Rabbi Akiva, that you have been seized for busying yourself with the Torah! Alas for Pappus who has been seized for busying himself with foolishness!"

When Rabbi Akiva was taken out for execution, it was the hour for the recital of the Shema (the traditional declaration of faith in God), and while they combed his flesh with iron combs, he recited the prayer. His disciples said to him: "Our teacher, even this far (i.e., Must one pray even when undergoing such tortures)?" He said to them: "All my days I have been troubled by this verse, 'You shall love the Lord your God with all your soul,' which means even if God takes your soul. I said: 'When shall I be able to fulfill this?' Now that I have the opportunity, shall I not fulfill it?" He prolonged the word "One" until he died. A voice came out of heaven and said: "Happy are you, Akiva."

Akiva's parable tells us that living without faith is its own death, comparable to a fish living on land. Perhaps Akiva would still breathe, but life would be worthless. Loss of life is less in the end than loss of a reason to live. With his last declaration he made clear that what he sought was not more time but more meaning for the time he had been given.

If you do not know what you are willing to die for, wrote

Martin Luther King, Jr., then you are not fit to live. Death is a loss, but to live without meaning is a kind of death, and in its way a greater loss, because it is a negation of life.

"The grasshopper also has a lesson to teach to us. All the summer through it sings, until its belly bursts, and death claims it. Though it knows the fate that awaits it, it sings on." Though the entomology may be inaccurate, the philosophy is clear. The meaning of death consists not in death itself, but in the life attitude we take—in knowing that death will strike and yet not allowing life to be rendered dismal and somber by that knowledge. Loss will be—should be—painful, for refusing to acknowledge loss is pathology, not piety. Yet it is in absorbing and transcending that knowledge that we become most fully human. The certainty that we will die should not cut short our song.

Death renders artistry possible, for art is the attempt to capture the instant in eternity. So Michelangelo implied when he said that "no thought exists in me which death has not carved with his chisel." Yet it was in defiance of death that his masterworks were created. Sculpting and painting were Michelangelo's ways of disputing the sovereignty of death. Everyone who lives successfully finds a way both to acknowledge death and, in some measure, to overcome it.

Part of the truth of loss is that without the pain, without the feeling that it is not worth it, the lessons are not learned. When my grandmother tried to throw herself into her sister's grave, she did not want wisdom. She wanted her sister back. In time we can appreciate the lessons to be learned. At the moment, we cry out for what we once had.

If our reaction to loss ends with that cry, we have lost twice— both the actual loss and the possibility of growing from it.

Growth does not happen right away, not while we are in the coils of loss. It takes time.

So we hold life dear, knowing that it will betray us. Hemingway wrote that every true story ends in death. We all live true stories, and that knowledge is ever at the edge of consciousness.

Why, then, do we reach for meaning in this life? Why do we not devote ourselves exclusively to the possibility, the hope, of something beyond? The central concern of faith is not how to escape death but how to sanctify life. We do not know what will come after. While we live in this world, the wiser search not for immortality but for sanctity.

Because death is the greatest loss, it harbors the greatest lessons. All along the way, we are constantly learning, and knowing that life must end cannot stop the process. After the novelist Isaac Bashevis Singer won the Nobel prize, he was asked why he writes in Yiddish, which, after all, is a dying language. Singer smiled and answered: "You are quite right, Yiddish is a dying language. But in Jewish history, the distance between dying and dead is very great." In all our lives, mortality is a condition of life, not a current reality. To live without recognizing both—that life will end but that it must be treasured while it exists—is to sacrifice life's preciousness for an illusion.

Human beings can do better. As Homer teaches in *The Iliad,* "The fates have given mortals hearts that can endure."

Our humanity is expressed most fully when we stake our souls in life, knowing that there is death. We love, even though we know that the beloved cannot live forever. We create, although we realize that all creation will decay. To be fully human is to stand before death, not ignoring it but not allowing it to undermine the meaning of the time we are given. There were orchestras in Auschwitz. The musicians knew death intimately—the stench of death surrounded them. Still they created beauty amid destruction because they knew that to believe in the possibility of wonder, of music, of radiance, was what kept them human.

"I am going to live with the fear," Linda said, "and I am going to *really* live in spite of it."

Notes

The notes below are not comprehensive, and several quotations in the text appear without citations. I tried to track down those statements that floated around in my memory or in my notebooks as best I could, but this is a work of advocacy and inspiration, not scholarship, and so I rested content with the sources I could find. The notes are for those who wish to explore certain matters further. Talmudic citations are from the Babylonian Talmud unless otherwise noted.

Chapter 1: Making Loss Matter

page 1 . . . *discovered that he was dying.* Ernest Becker, *The Denial of Death* (New York: Free Press, 1973).

page 6 . . . *signposts to their descendants.* See Ramban's introduction to *parashat* Vayishlach.

page 16 . . . *Aaron hears the voice of God.* Leviticus 10:8. When Aaron's sons die five verses earlier, Aaron's reaction is significant: "And Aaron was silent." There are losses that defy explanation or discussion, times in our lives when the only reaction true to the moment is silence.

Chapter 2: Home

page 23 "... *something that you lose.*" Quoted in Lawrence Langer's *Holocaust Testimonies* (New Haven: Yale University Press, 1991), p. 191.

page 28 ... *they do not know they will die.* Compare the protagonist in Sartre's short story "The Wall," who is to be executed the next morning and suddenly realizes, "I had lived as if I had forever."

page 33 *Once the cord snaps, he will die.* See Louis Ginzburg, *Legends of the Jews*, vol. 1 (Philadelphia: Jewish Publication Society, 1968), p. 31.

page 40 *The only true paradises are those we have lost.* See Marcel Proust, *Cities of the Plain*, trans. C. K. Scott Moncrieff and Terence Kilmartin (New York: Random House, 1981), p. 888. The idealization of childhood in life and literature is almost always recounted in the voice of the adult. When a child speaks, the voice is more measured, recounting the pain as well as the delights of youth.

page 40 "... *a veil between us.*" Erich Maria Remarque, *All Quiet on the Western Front* (New York: Ballantine Books, 1996), p. 160.

page 45 ... *always seeks home.* One could argue, of course, that the vividness of Homer's depiction of Odysseus gave rise to the tale of Homer's wandering. Often enough the power of an imaginative writer's description gives rise to speculation about the progress of his own life. We simply do not know.

page 46 ... *holy man of Jerusalem.* His inspiring story is told in *A Tzaddik in Our Time: The Life of Rabbi Aryeh Levin*, by Simcha Raz (New York: Feldheim, 1989).

page 48 *The Chofetz Chaim* ..."Chofetz Chaim" was a pen name, taken from Psalm 34, for Rabbi Israel Mayer Kahan, 1838–1933. The psalm asks who desires life (in Hebrew: *chofetz chaim*) and answers with the advice "Keep your tongue from evil and your lips from deceit." The Chofetz Chaim wrote a number of books on piety, with a special emphasis on proper speech.

Chapter 3: Dreams

page 54 ... *hardscrabble reality of the world.* See the comment by Ramban, who cannot understand the purpose of Jacob's remark (Ramban on Gen. 47:9). What good does it do for him to complain to the ruler of Egypt about the hardships of his life? Yet there is in Jacob's attitude something Graham Greene says of a character in his novel *The Heart of the Matter* (New York: Penguin Books, 1991), p. 166: "He felt the loy-alty we feel to unhappiness—the sense that that is where we really belong." Jacob's unhappiness rings true in his character, not only for the hardship of his life but for the substance of his soul.

page 55 . . . *but Jacob leaves* (va-yetze). See Avivah Zornberg, *Genesis: The Beginning of Desire* (Philadelphia: Jewish Publication Society, 1995), p. 180.

page 60 . . . *Jacob himself?* The interpretation that Jacob wrestled with an angel is given by Rabbinic Midrash. See, for example, Bereshit Rabbah 77:2, 78:6, and Song of Songs Rabbah 3:6. Nahum Sarna argues that the assailant is the "celestial patron of Esau-Edom." See Bereshit Genesis in the Jewish Publication Society Torah commentary (Philadelphia, 1989).

page 70 . . . *more than three decades.* See the interesting essay "Darwin's Delay" on this theme by Steven Jay Gould in *Ever Since Darwin* (New York: W. W. Norton & Co., 1977).

page 71 . . . *no one would die.* T. Carmi, "Out of Luck," in *The Penguin Book of Hebrew Verse* (New York and Philadelphia: Penguin Books and Jewish Publication Society, 1981, 1997), p. 353.

page 72 . . . *has not failed in it.* Gittin 43a.

page 73 *He had faith.* These examples come from *Churchill: A Life*, by Martin Gilbert (New York: Henry Holt & Co., 1991).

page 74 . . . *turned to benefit.* See the article "Worst Practices" in *Gartner Group Technology* magazine, December 1998. I am indebted to Mark Schwartz for calling this article to my attention.

page 77 *". . . as I have not yet done."* Cited in Paul Johnson, *History of the English People* (New York: Harper and Row, 1972), p. 56.

page 78 . . . *from under his stove.* Martin Buber's lesson from this episode is that the fulfillment of existence is where one stands. For Buber it is a call to immediacy and authenticity.

page 79 *". . . governed by young men."* Marc Bloch, *The Feudal Society*, trans. L. A. Manyon (Chicago: University of Chicago Press, 1961), pp. 72 – 73.

page 81 *". . . as they did before the war."* Arthur Green, *Tormented Master: A Life of Rabbi Nahman of Bratslav* (University, AL: University of Alabama Press, 1976).

page 82 *". . . who will come after me."* Ta'anit 23.

Chapter 4: Self

page 86 . . . *chronicle of a loss of self.* The story of Saul is told in I Samuel, chapter 9.

page 88 ". . . *for the other's ideas."* Henrik Ibsen, *Peer Gynt,* Act IV, Scene 13. Text available at the English Server, http://eserver.org/drama/ peer.gynt.txt.

page 95 ". . . *against official goodness."* Carlos Baker, *Emerson Among the Eccentrics* (New York: Viking, 1996), p. 14.

page 95 . . . *discovery by loss.* See Lionel Trilling's *The Liberal Imagination* (New York: Harcourt Brace Jovanovich, 1979), pp. 21–32. Anderson's work was defined by that moment, according to Trilling: the contest between freedom and subjugation or, in our terms, between the exile that helps define the self and the entrapment that obscures it.

page 97 ". . . *afraid to do."* Robert Richardson, *Emerson: The Mind on Fire* (Berkeley: University of California Press, 1995), p. 25.

page 114 . . . *inside the human heart.* I heard this legend from Rabbi Edward Feinstein.

page 115 . . . *poet and mystic Novalis.* For a full and fascinating exegesis of this theme, see Charles Taylor's *Sources of the Self* (Cambridge, MA: Harvard University Press, 1992).

Chapter 5: Love

page 122 . . . *a stratagem of the life force.* For a popular take on the current speculations of evolutionary biology on this point, see Robert Wright, *The Moral Animal* (New York: Vintage, 1995). Also Emerson, often thought of as airily dismissive of hard realities, once remarked to Margaret Fuller that "love was only phenomenal, a contrivance of nature" (see Carlos Baker, *Emerson Among the Eccentrics,* p. xii).

page 132 . . . *an Isaac complex.* See E. Wellisch, *Isaac and Oedipus* (London: Routledge & Kegan Paul, 1954). Also, Carol Delaney, *Abraham on Trial: The Social Legacy of Biblical Myth* (Princeton, NJ: Princeton University Press, 1998).

page 132 . . . *destructive impluses.* The famed psychoanalyst and pediatrician D. W. Winnicott lists eighteen reasons why all loving mothers hate their babies. Cited in Judith Viorst, *Necessary Losses* (New York: Ballantine Books, 1986), p. 66. Viorst's book is an engaging and insightful discussion of many of the issues of loss, with an extensive bibliography.

page 133 " '. . . *lodged me in prison.' "* Ben ha-Melek 6, in Ginzburg, *Legends of the Jews,* vol. 5, pp. 369, 370, note 400.

page 134 . . . *suffers at the end as well.* Ivan Turgenev, *First Love,* trans. Isaiah

Berlin (New York: Penguin Books, 1979), pp. 52, 97. Werther details the anguish of unrequited love, as does much (though hardly all) of Proust. But even requited love is hardly smooth and untroubled, in life or literature. The whole Proust can be characterized as an extended paean to the difficulties, anguishes, and obstacles of and to love. De Rougemont writes that "happy love has no history." The secret de Rougemont finds in European Romantic literature is not unrequited love but "unhappy mutual love." See de Rougemont's *Love in the Western World* (New York: Pantheon, 1956), p. 15.

page 140 *"The man that loved me died."* "The Colonel's Lady" is one of four stories contained in *Quartet* (New York: Avon, 1949). The book also contains the screenplays of each story, which were subsequently made into a movie. Interestingly, the short story itself ends with the line "What in the name of heaven did the fellow ever see in her?" and the screenplay, by R. C. Sherriff, ends as described here.

page 142 *". . . rather than with my children."* Winston Churchill, *History of the English-Speaking People*, vol. 3 (New York: Dorset Press, 1956).

Chapter 6: Faith

page 153 *". . . everyone believes it."* I read through Russell's popular books, especially *Why I Am Not a Christian* (London: Unwin, 1957), for his views on faith and doubt. Some of his most telling aperçus were collected in *The Best of Bertrand Russell* (London: Unwin, 1958).

page 156 *" '. . . never to let go of his hand.' "* Rose Farkas, *Ruchele: Sixty Years from Szatmar to Los Angeles* (Santa Barbara: Fithian Press, 1998).

page 160 *"Friendship or death"* Ta'anit 23a.

page 162 *" '. . . able to go on.' "* Elie Wiesel, *Four Hasidic Masters* (Notre Dame, IN: University of Notre Dame Press, 1978), pp. 2, 3.

page 164 *He asks if Job . . .* The question of God's gender crosses literary into theological boundaries. Theologically, God has no gender, so He or She is not properly applied. In the Hebrew text, however, God is referred to as He, a practice we have adopted here for fluency, despite the conceptual distortion in implying God is male.

page 164 *. . . the interpretations of the book.* There is an enormous literature on the book of Job. The interpretation followed here is developed by Matitahu Tsevat in his book *The Meaning of the Book of Job and Other Biblical Studies* (New York: K'tav, 1980).

page 165 *. . . as one does for good things.* Berachot 33b.

page 173 . . *see God gradually recede:* . . . See Richard Elliott Friedman, *The Hidden Face of God* (San Francisco: Harper SanFrancisco, 1997).

page 176 *"The prophets do not speak* . . . "For the quotations from Heschel and a survey of the topic of God's hiddenness, see my "Hester Panim in Modern Jewish Thought" in *Modern Judaism* 17 (1997)

page 179 *". . . make it a Soul?"* Lionel Trilling, ed., *The Selected Letters of John Keats* (New York: Farrar Straus, 1951), p. 215.

Chapter 7: Life

page 186 *My Memoirs*, by Alexandre Dumas, is quoted in D. J. Enright, ed., *The Oxford Book of Death* (New York: Oxford University Press, 1983).

page 192 *One death, two legacies.* William Trevor, *The Stories of William Trevor* (New York: Viking, 1992).

page 198 . . . *thinking he is reversing course* . . . Jacques Choron, *Death and Western Thought* (London: Collier-Macmillan, 1963), p. 211.

page 203 . . . *the moment we are born.* The Talmud repeats a version of the same legend, teaching that each person has a comprehensive knowledge of Torah until, right before birth, an angel comes along and wipes out the prenatal memory. Then we are born. See Niddah 30b.

page 204 . . . *we will live on.* A recent book that summarizes the various Jewish views of the afterlife is *The Death of Death: Resurrection and Immortality in Jewish Thought*, by Neil Gillman (Woodstock, VT: Jewish Lights, 1997). The story about twins in a womb is found in the standard Hebrew work on Jewish mourning, *Gesher Hachayim* (The Bridge of Life), by R. Tukachinsky.

page 204 *". . . I was young."* Jose Luis Borges, *Other Inquisitions* (Austin, TX: University of Texas Press, 1964), p. 71.

page 205 *". . . a dead man's best memorial."* Michael Alexander, ed., *Beowulf* (New York: Penguin Books, 1995), section 21.

page 208 . . . *the time after we die.* Vladimir Nabokov, *Speak Memory* (New York: Putnam, 1966), p. 19.

page 211 *". . . 'Happy are you, Akiva.' "* Berachot 61b (author's translation, abridged).

page 211 *". . . it sings on."* Louis Ginzburg, *Legends of the Jews*, vol. 1, p. 43.

page 212 *". . . carved with his chisel."* Quoted in Elisabeth Kübler-Ross, *Death: The Final Stage of Growth* (Englewood Cliffs, NJ: Prentice-Hall, 1975).

page 213 . . . *but for sanctity.* Jack Riemer, ed., "Death as Homecoming," in *Jewish Reflections on Death* (New York: Schocken, 1974).

page 213 *". . . that can endure."* Homer, *The Iliad*, trans. Robert Fagles (New York: Penguin Books, 1991), book 2.

Acknowledgments

I would like to thank my editor, Amy Hertz, for her skill and support, and also a number of people who graciously helped along the way: Lynn Nesbit, Cullen Stanley, Robert Wexler, Shai Held, Marilyn Goldman, Jan Zakowski, and my many friends at Sinai Temple. I am grateful to the students, congregants, and friends who have shared their stories with me. My deepest thanks go to Samara, who missed her daddy on many mornings when his time was claimed by writing and rewriting, and to Eliana, for her bracing criticism, her expansive spirit, and her love.

Index